Enjoy Learning How to Draw Animals!

An Exciting Activity Book

BOBO's Children Activity Books

COLORING, DRAWING & ACTIVITY BOOKS FOR CHILDREN

Copyright 2016

All Rights reserved. No part of this book may be reproduced or used in any way or formor by any means whether electronic or mechanical, this means that you cannot recordor photocopy any material ideas or tips that are provided in this book.

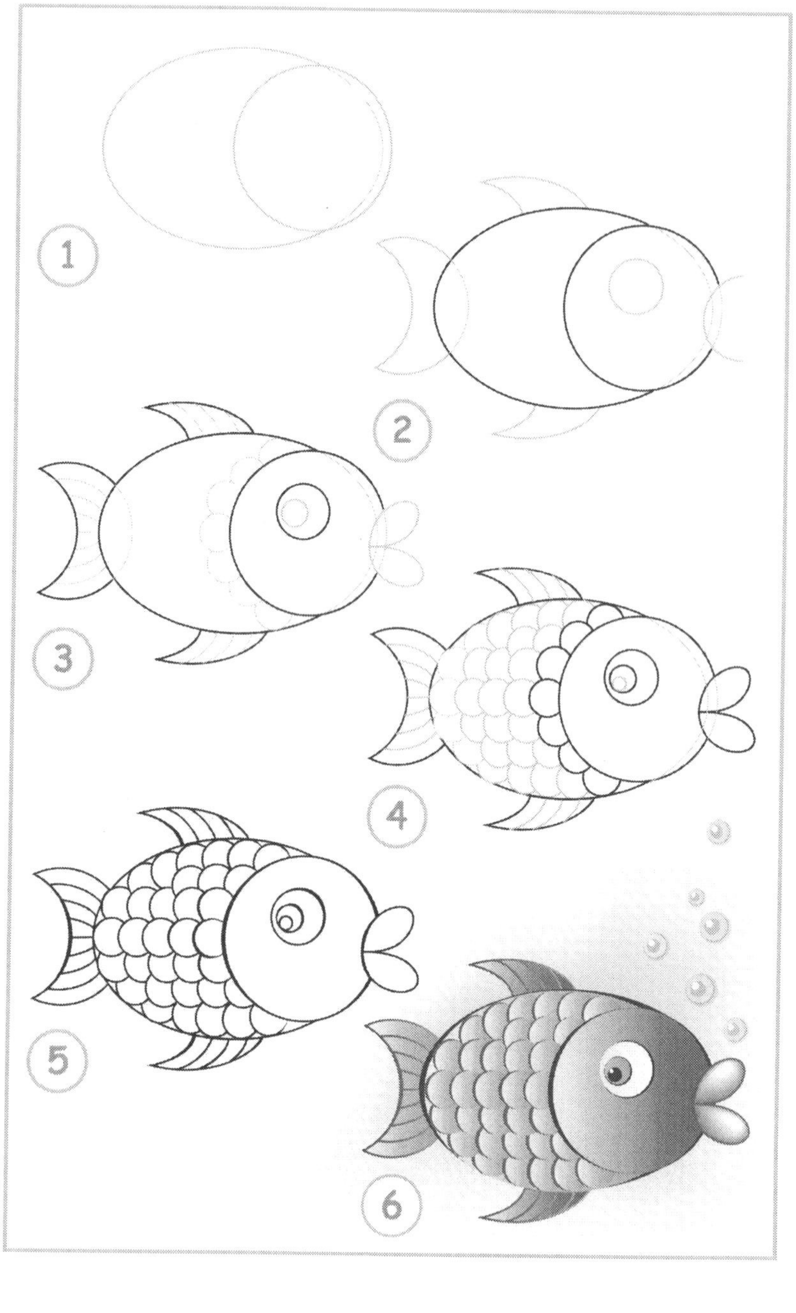
1
2
3
4
5
6

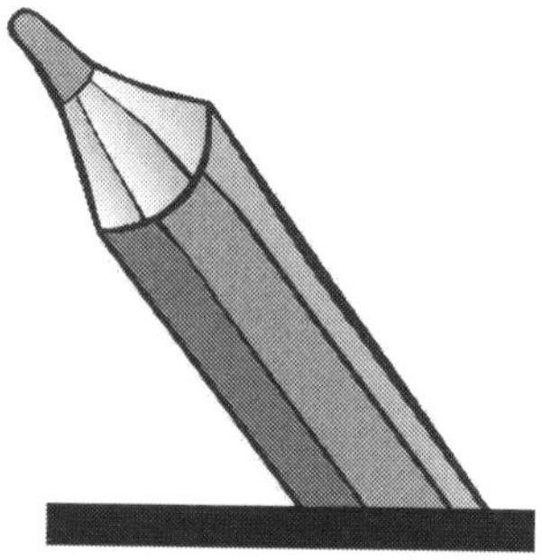

This is a Bleed Through Page If You Are Using a Coloring Marker or Pen!
Find Other Great Titles By searching for BoBo's Children Activity Books on Your Favorite Book Retailer
Amazon.Com | Barnes & Noble (BN.Com) | Books A Million (BAM.Com)

BOBO's
CHILDREN ACTIVITY BOOKS
COLORING, DRAWING & ACTIVITY BOOKS FOR CHILDREN

1
2
3
4
5
6

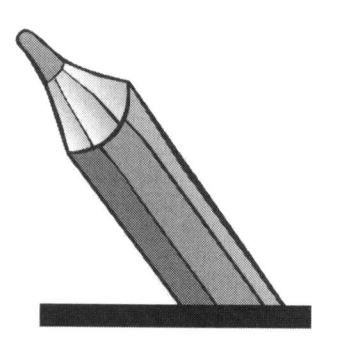

This is a Bleed Through Page If You Are Using a Coloring Marker or Pen!
Find Other Great Titles By searching for BoBo's Children Activity Books on Your Favorite Book Retailer
Amazon.Com | Barnes & Noble (BN.Com) | Books A Million (BAM.Com)

BOBO's
CHILDREN ACTIVITY BOOKS
COLORING, DRAWING & ACTIVITY BOOKS FOR CHILDREN

1 2 3 4 5 6

This is a Bleed Through Page If You Are Using a Coloring Marker or Pen!
Find Other Great Titles By searching for BoBo's Children Activity Books on Your Favorite Book Retailer
Amazon.Com | Barnes & Noble (BN.Com) | Books A Million (BAM.Com)

BOBO's
CHILDREN ACTIVITY BOOKS
COLORING, DRAWING & ACTIVITY BOOKS FOR CHILDREN

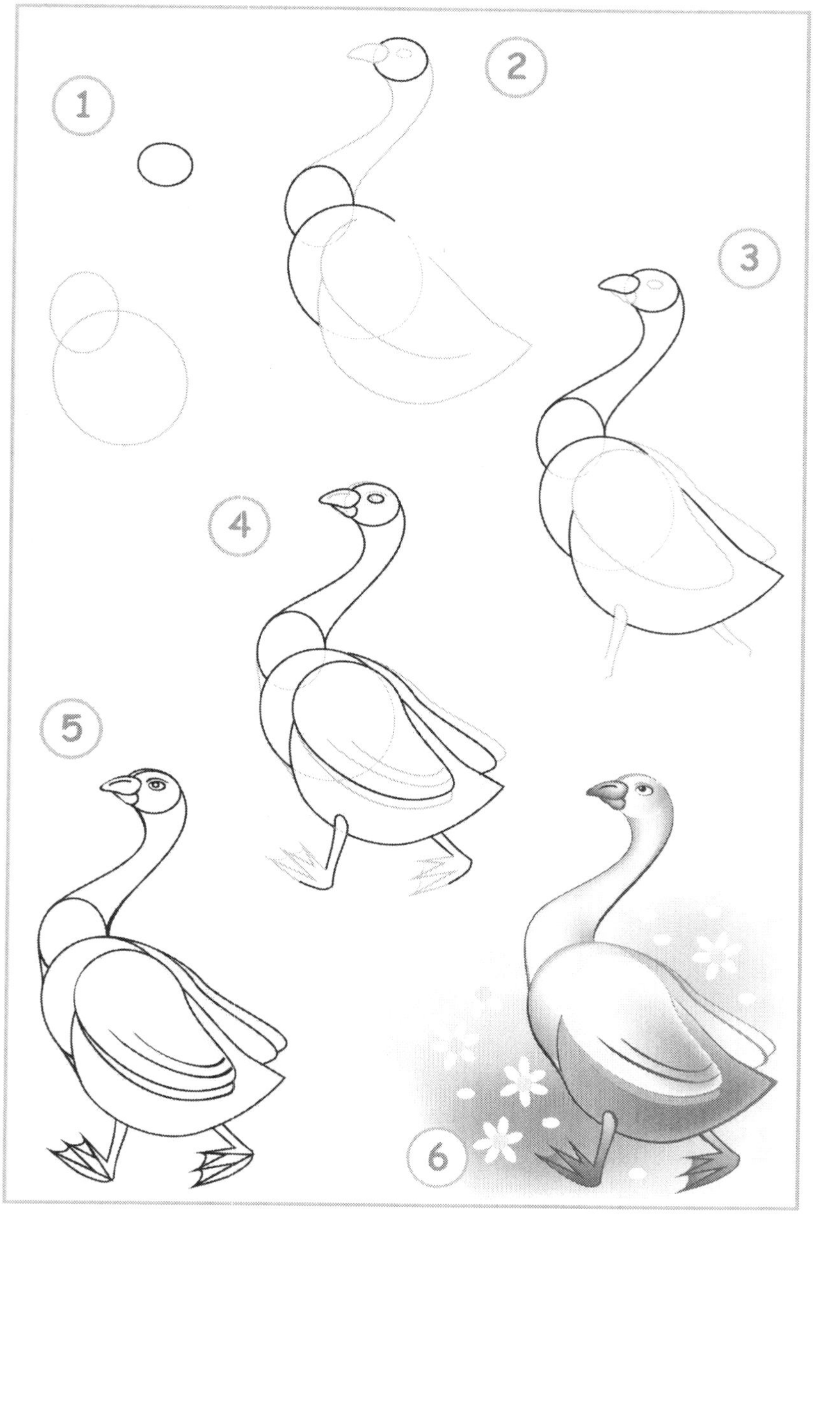
1
2
3
4
5
6

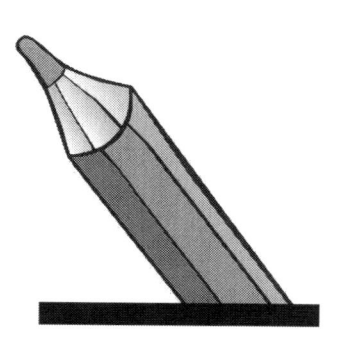

This is a Bleed Through Page If You Are Using a Coloring Marker or Pen!
Find Other Great Titles By searching for BoBo's Children Activity Books on Your Favorite Book Retailer
Amazon.Com | Barnes & Noble (BN.Com) | Books A Million (BAM.Com)

BOBO's
CHILDREN ACTIVITY BOOKS
COLORING, DRAWING & ACTIVITY BOOKS FOR CHILDREN

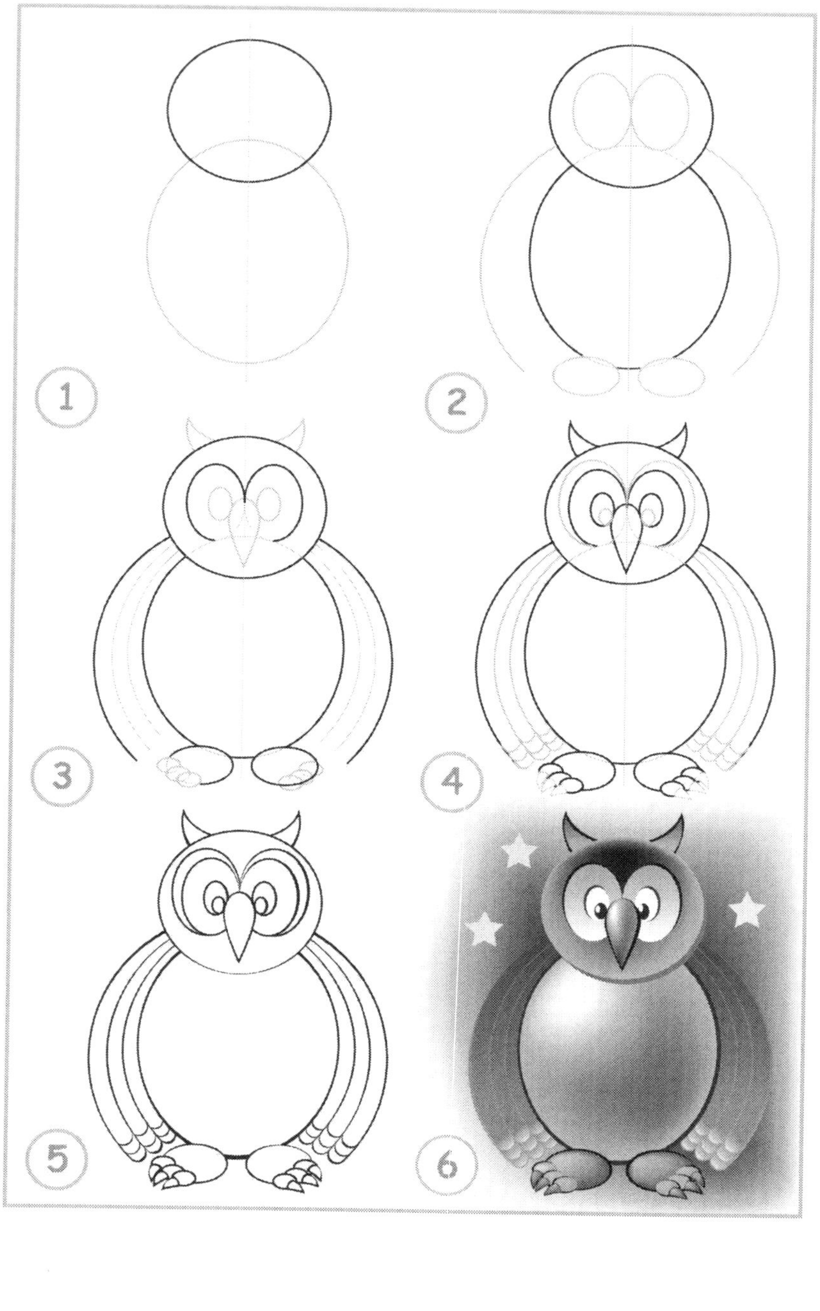
1
2
3
4
5
6

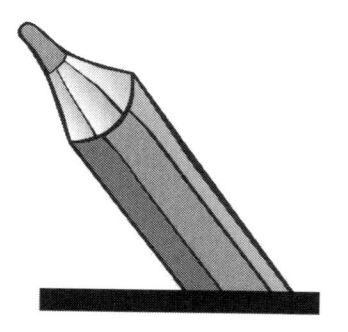

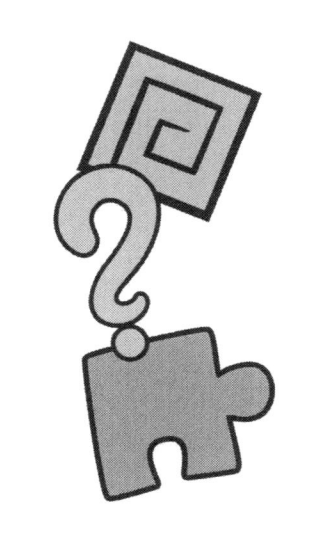

This is a Bleed Through Page If You Are Using a Coloring Marker or Pen!
Find Other Great Titles By searching for BoBo's Children Activity Books on Your Favorite Book Retailer
Amazon.Com | Barnes & Noble (BN.Com) | Books A Million (BAM.Com)

BOBO's
CHILDREN ACTIVITY BOOKS
COLORING, DRAWING & ACTIVITY BOOKS FOR CHILDREN

① ② ③ ④ ⑤ ⑥

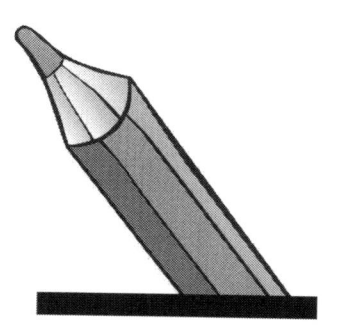

This is a Bleed Through Page If You Are Using a Coloring Marker or Pen!
Find Other Other Great Titles By searching for BoBo's Children Activity Books on Your Favorite Book Retailer
Amazon.Com | Barnes & Noble (BN.Com) | Books A Million (BAM.Com)

BOBO's
CHILDREN ACTIVITY BOOKS
COLORING, DRAWING & ACTIVITY BOOKS FOR CHILDREN

1
2
3
4
5
6

This is a Bleed Through Page If You Are Using a Coloring Marker or Pen!
Find Other Great Titles By searching for BoBo's Children Activity Books on Your Favorite Book Retailer
Amazon.Com | Barnes & Noble (BN.Com) | Books A Million (BAM.Com)

BOBO's
CHILDREN ACTIVITY BOOKS
COLORING, DRAWING & ACTIVITY BOOKS FOR CHILDREN

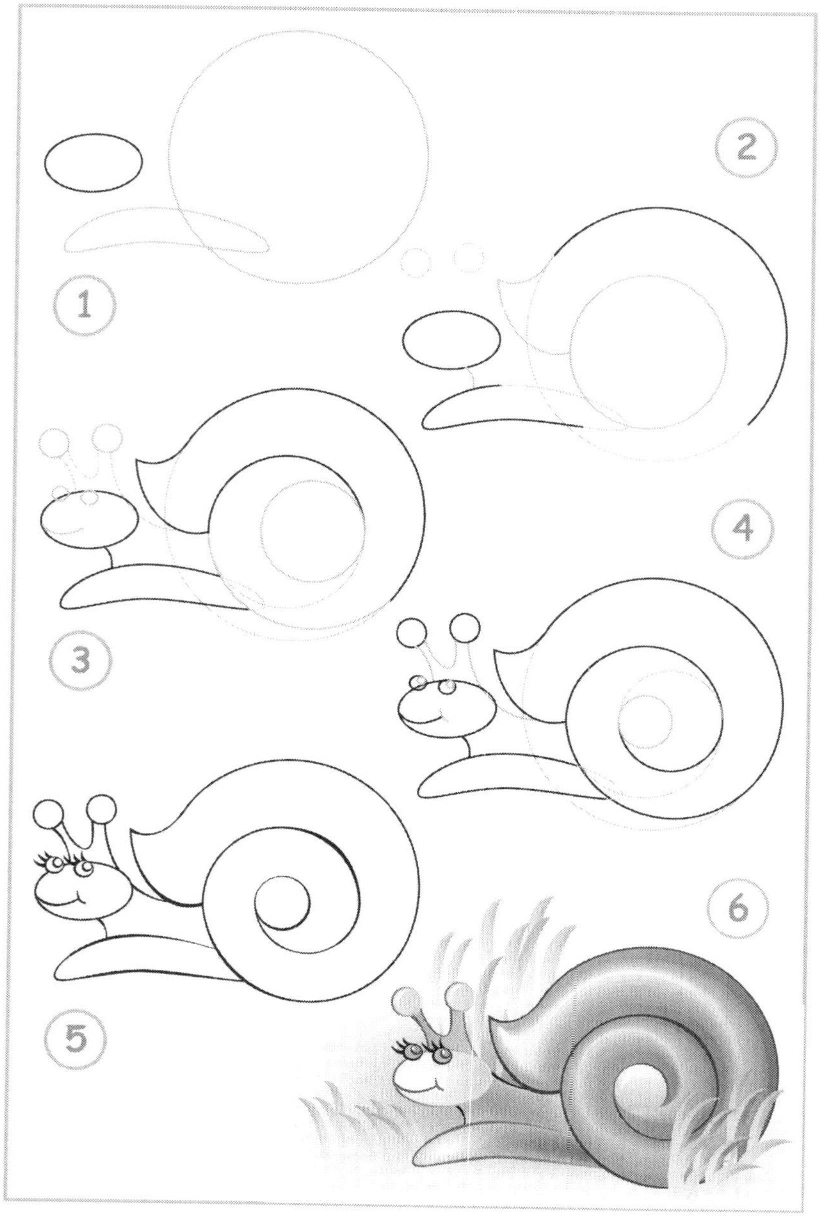
1
2
3
4
5
6
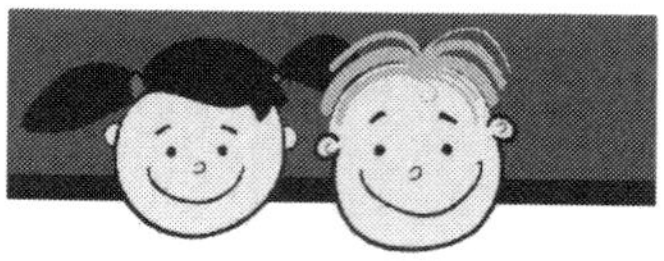

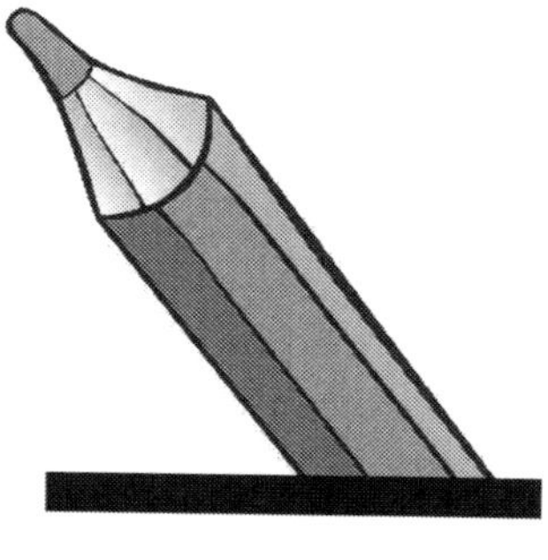

This is a Bleed Through Page If You Are Using a Coloring Marker or Pen!
Find Other Great Titles By searching for <u>*BoBo's Children Activity Books*</u> *on Your Favorite Book Retailer*
Amazon.Com | Barnes & Noble (BN.Com) | Books A Million (BAM.Com)

BOBO's
CHILDREN ACTIVITY BOOKS
COLORING, DRAWING & ACTIVITY BOOKS FOR CHILDREN

① ② ③ ④ ⑤ ⑥

This is a Bleed Through Page If You Are Using a Coloring Marker or Pen!
Find Other Great Titles By searching for BoBo's Children Activity Books *on Your Favorite Book Retailer*
Amazon.Com | Barnes & Noble (BN.Com) | Books A Million (BAM.Com)

BOBO's
CHILDREN ACTIVITY BOOKS
COLORING, DRAWING & ACTIVITY BOOKS FOR CHILDREN

1
2
3
4
5
6

This is a Bleed Through Page If You Are Using a Coloring Marker or Pen!
Find Other Great Titles By searching for BoBo's Children Activity Books *on Your Favorite Book Retailer*
Amazon.Com | Barnes & Noble (BN.Com) | Books A Million (BAM.Com)

BOBO's
CHILDREN ACTIVITY BOOKS
COLORING, DRAWING & ACTIVITY BOOKS FOR CHILDREN

1 2
3 4
5 6

This is a Bleed Through Page If You Are Using a Coloring Marker or Pen!
Find Other Great Titles By searching for BoBo's Children Activity Books on Your Favorite Book Retailer
Amazon.Com | Barnes & Noble (BN.Com) | Books A Million (BAM.Com)

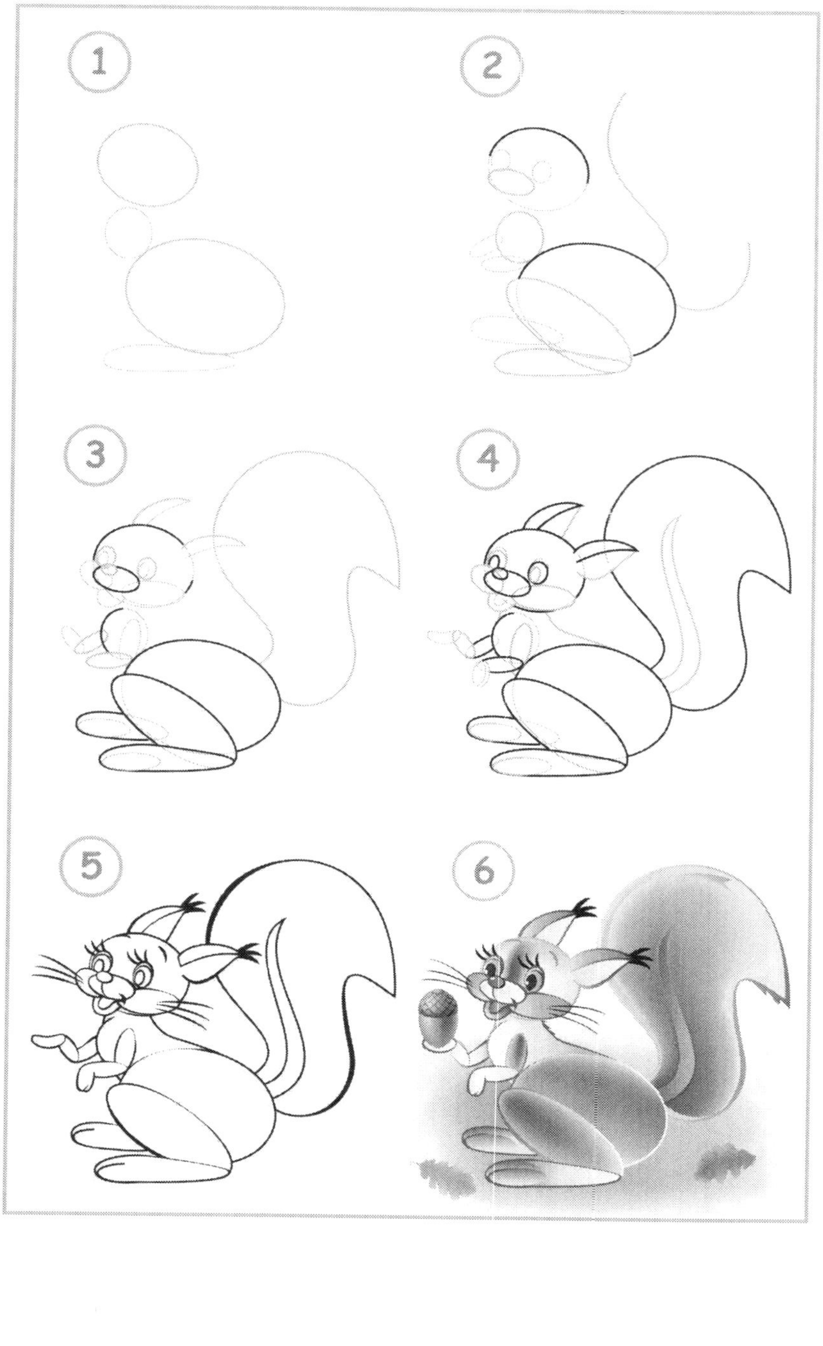
1
2
3
4
5
6

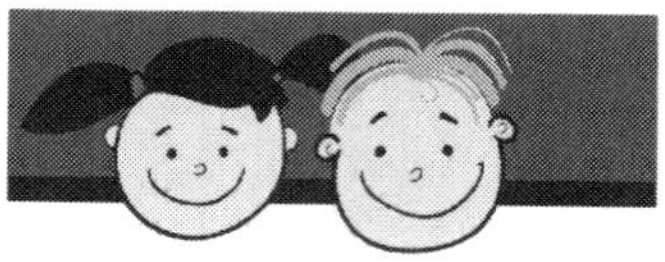

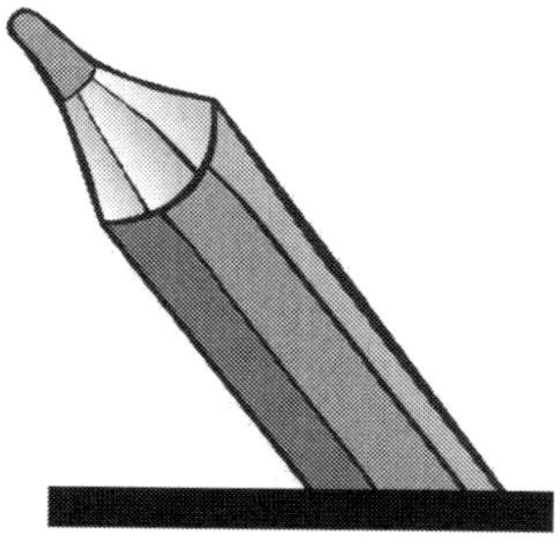

This is a Bleed Through Page If You Are Using a Coloring Marker or Pen!
Find Other Great Titles By searching for BoBo's Children Activity Books *on Your Favorite Book Retailer*
Amazon.Com | Barnes & Noble (BN.Com) | Books A Million (BAM.Com)

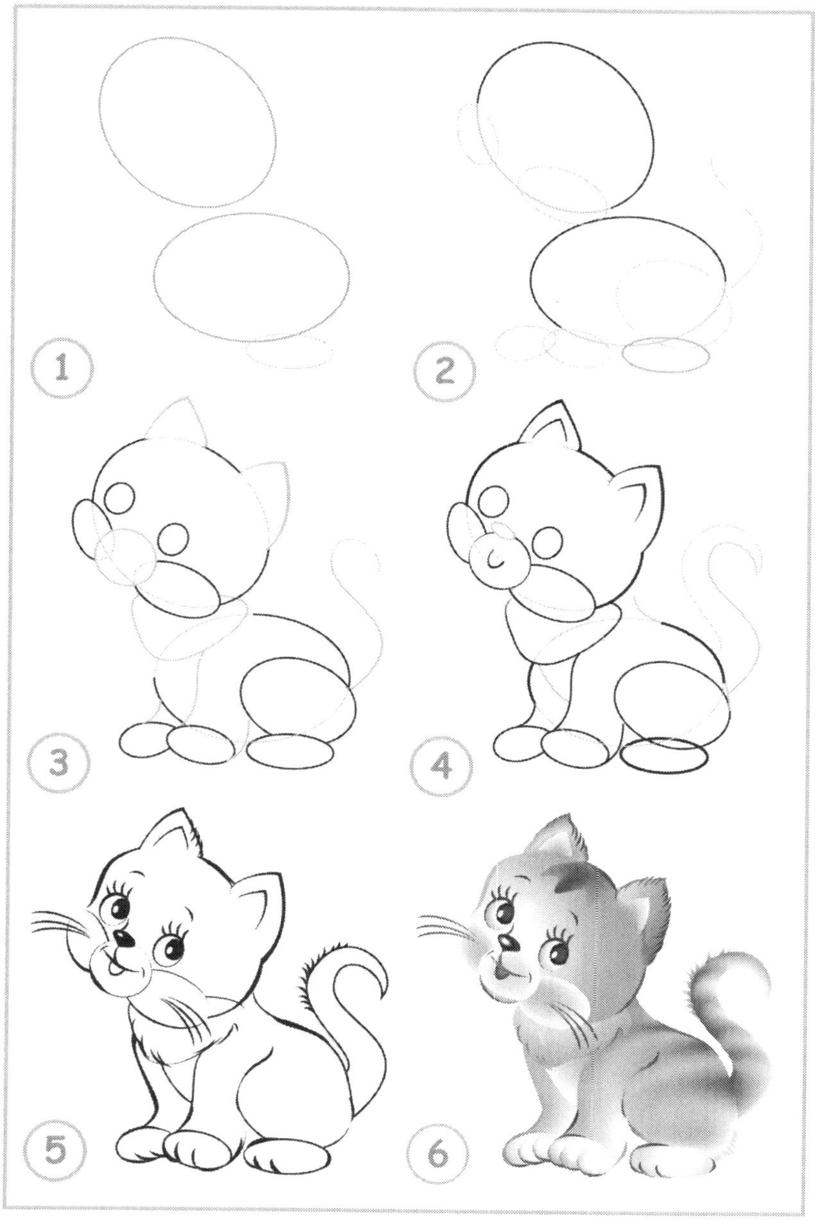
1
2
3
4
5
6

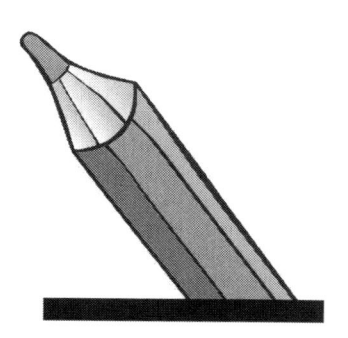

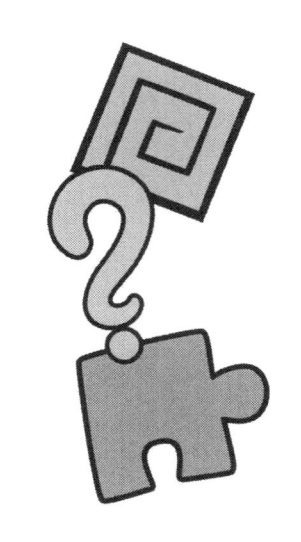

This is a Bleed Through Page If You Are Using a Coloring Marker or Pen!
Find Other Great Titles By searching for BoBo's Children Activity Books on Your Favorite Book Retailer
Amazon.Com | Barnes & Noble (BN.Com) | Books A Million (BAM.Com)

BOBO's
CHILDREN ACTIVITY BOOKS
COLORING, DRAWING & ACTIVITY BOOKS FOR CHILDREN

1
2
3
4
5
6

This is a Bleed Through Page If You Are Using a Coloring Marker or Pen!
Find Other Great Titles By searching for BoBo's Children Activity Books *on Your Favorite Book Retailer*
Amazon.Com | Barnes & Noble (BN.Com) | Books A Million (BAM.Com)

① ② ③ ④ ⑤ ⑥

This is a Bleed Through Page If You Are Using a Coloring Marker or Pen!
Find Other Great Titles By searching for BoBo's Children Activity Books *on Your Favorite Book Retailer*
Amazon.Com | Barnes & Noble (BN.Com) | Books A Million (BAM.Com)

BOBO's
CHILDREN ACTIVITY BOOKS
COLORING, DRAWING & ACTIVITY BOOKS FOR CHILDREN

① ② ③ ④ ⑤ ⑥

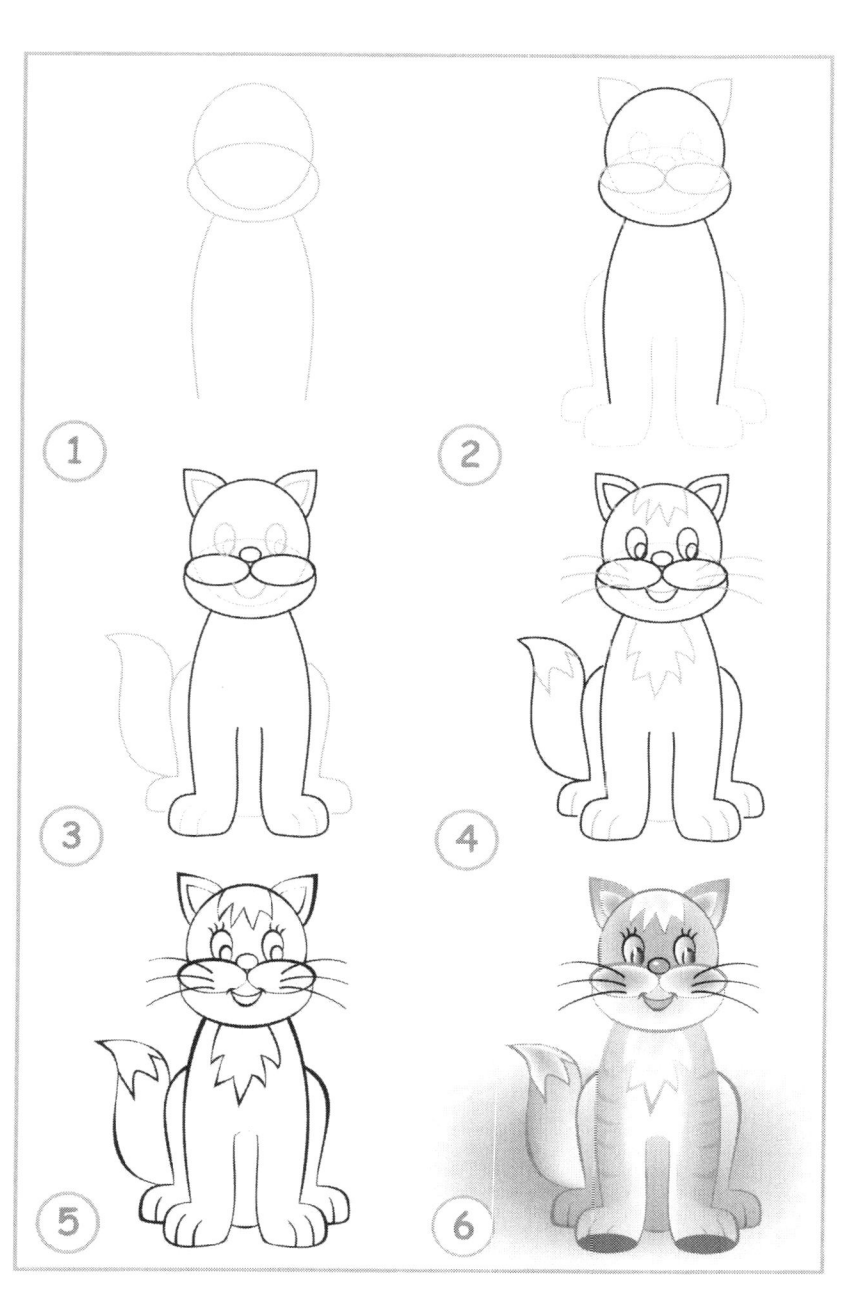

This is a Bleed Through Page If You Are Using a Coloring Marker or Pen!
Find Other Great Titles By searching for BoBo's Children Activity Books *on Your Favorite Book Retailer*
Amazon.Com | Barnes & Noble (BN.Com) | Books A Million (BAM.Com)

BOBO's
CHILDREN ACTIVITY BOOKS
COLORING, DRAWING & ACTIVITY BOOKS FOR CHILDREN

1
2
3
4
5
6

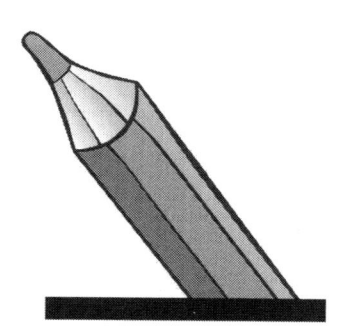

This is a Bleed Through Page If You Are Using a Coloring Marker or Pen!
Find Other Great Titles By searching for BoBo's Children Activity Books on Your Favorite Book Retailer
Amazon.Com | Barnes & Noble (BN.Com) | Books A Million (BAM.Com)

BoBo's
CHILDREN ACTIVITY BOOKS
COLORING, DRAWING & ACTIVITY BOOKS FOR CHILDREN

① ② ③ ④ ⑤ ⑥

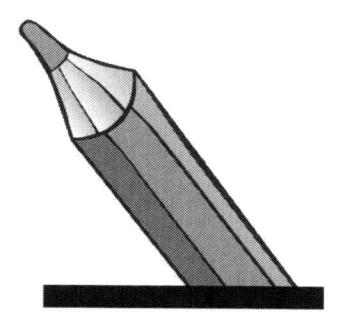

This is a Bleed Through Page If You Are Using a Coloring Marker or Pen!
Find Other Great Titles By searching for BoBo's Children Activity Books *on Your Favorite Book Retailer*
Amazon.Com | Barnes & Noble (BN.Com) | Books A Million (BAM.Com)

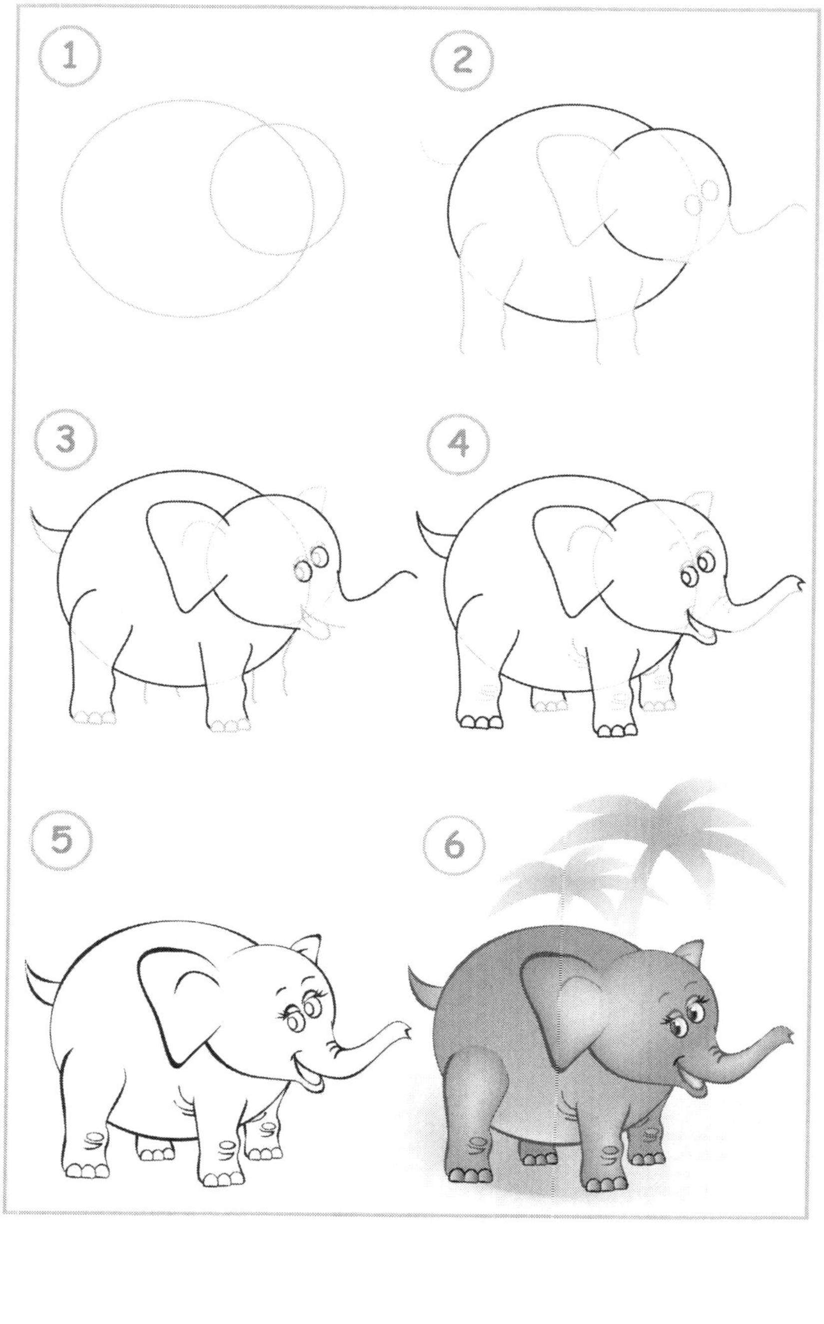
1
2
3
4
5
6

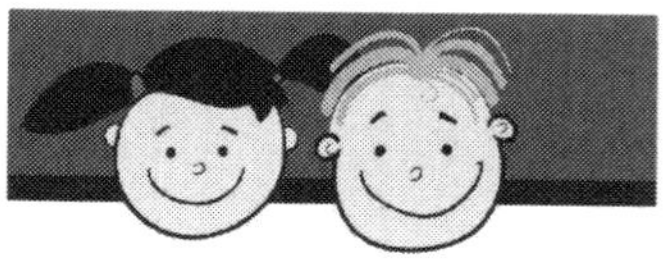

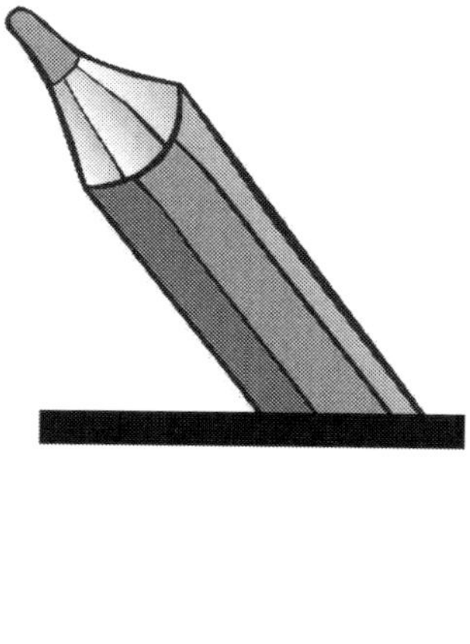

This is a Bleed Through Page If You Are Using a Coloring Marker or Pen!
Find Other Great Titles By searching for BoBo's Children Activity Books on Your Favorite Book Retailer
Amazon.Com | Barnes & Noble (BN.Com) | Books A Million (BAM.Com)

1 2 3 4 5 6

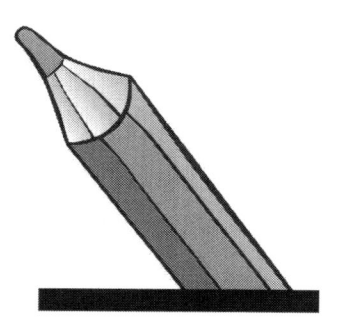

This is a Bleed Through Page If You Are Using a Coloring Marker or Pen!
Find Other Great Titles By searching for BoBo's Children Activity Books on Your Favorite Book Retailer
Amazon.Com | Barnes & Noble (BN.Com) | Books A Million (BAM.Com)

BOBO's
CHILDREN ACTIVITY BOOKS
COLORING, DRAWING & ACTIVITY BOOKS FOR CHILDREN

1
2
3
4
5
6

This is a Bleed Through Page If You Are Using a Coloring Marker or Pen!
Find Other Great Titles By searching for BoBo's Children Activity Books *on Your Favorite Book Retailer*
Amazon.Com | Barnes & Noble (BN.Com) | Books A Million (BAM.Com)

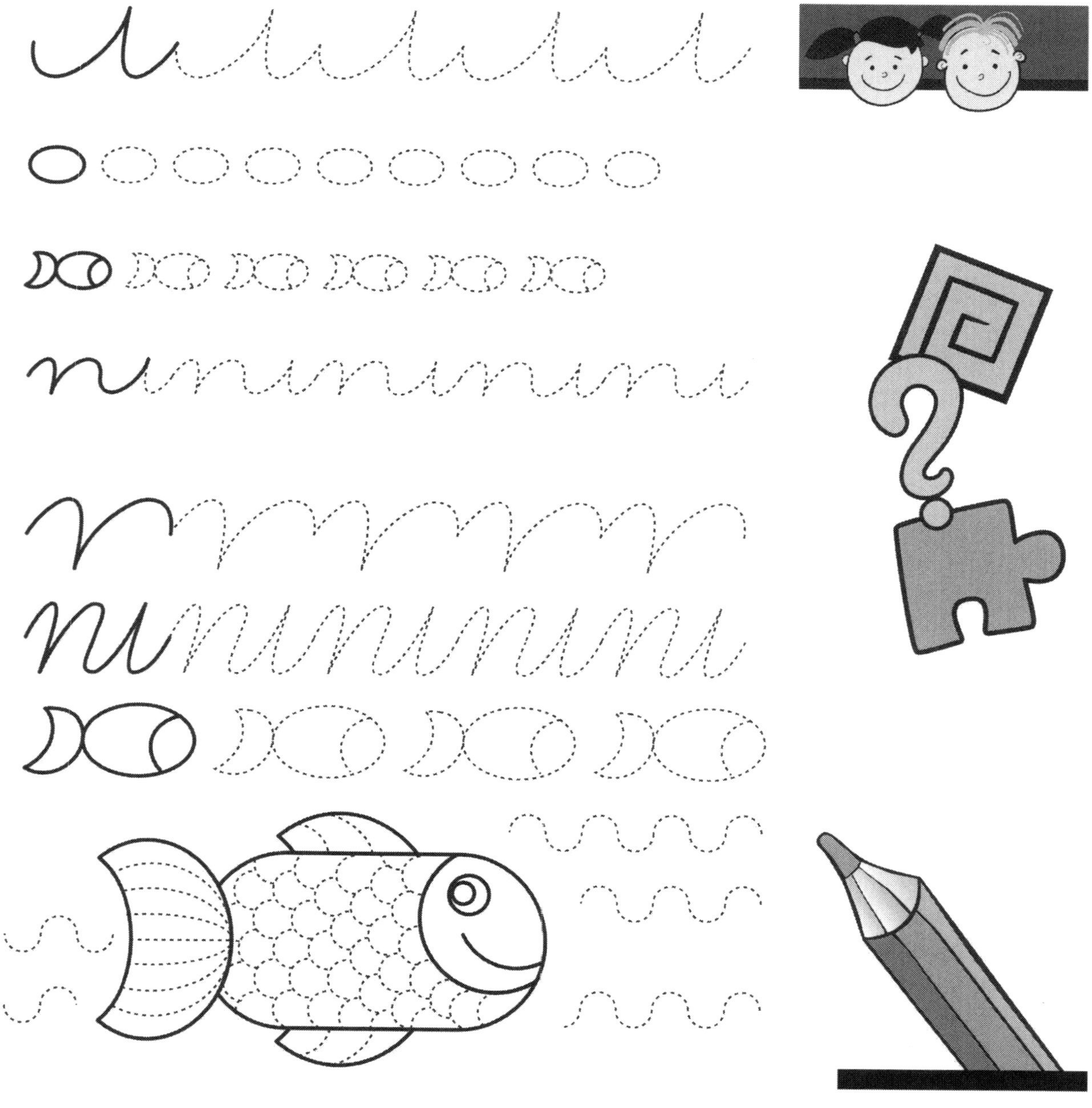

This is a Bleed Through Page If You Are Using a Coloring Marker or Pen!
Find Other Great Titles By searching for BoBo's Children Activity Books on Your Favorite Book Retailer
Amazon.Com | Barnes & Noble (BN.Com) | Books A Million (BAM.Com)

BOBO's
CHILDREN ACTIVITY BOOKS
COLORING, DRAWING & ACTIVITY BOOKS FOR CHILDREN

DRAW THE IMAGE

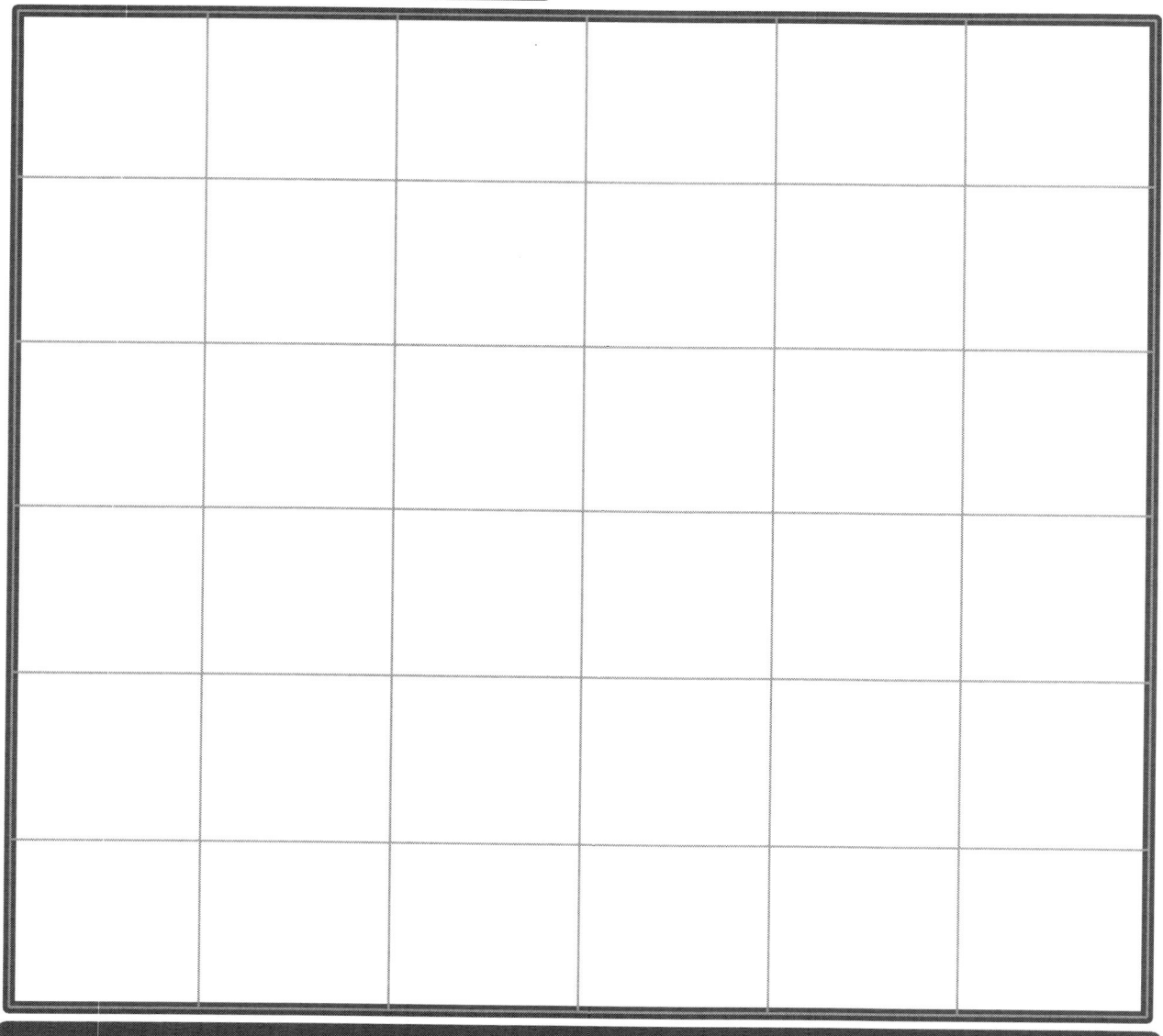

This is a Bleed Through Page If You Are Using a Coloring Marker or Pen!
Find Other Great Titles By searching for BoBo's Children Activity Books on Your Favorite Book Retailer
Amazon.Com | Barnes & Noble (BN.Com) | Books A Million (BAM.Com)

BOBO's CHILDREN ACTIVITY BOOKS

COLORING, DRAWING & ACTIVITY BOOKS FOR CHILDREN

DRAW
THE
IMAGE

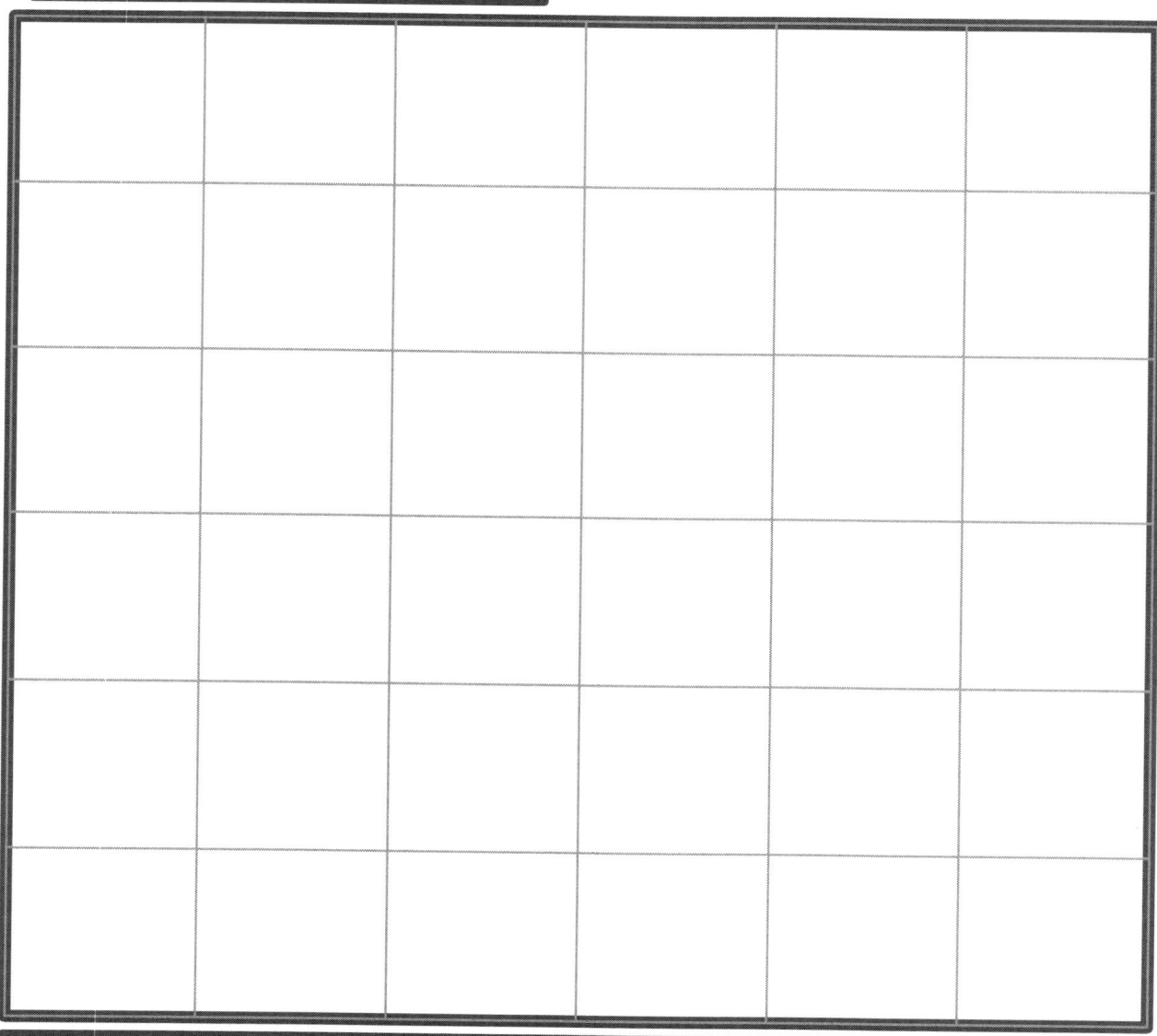

This is a Bleed Through Page If You Are Using a Coloring Marker or Pen!
Find Other Great Titles By searching for BoBo's Children Activity Books on Your Favorite Book Retailer
Amazon.Com | Barnes & Noble (BN.Com) | Books A Million (BAM.Com)

BoBo's
CHILDREN ACTIVITY BOOKS
COLORING, DRAWING & ACTIVITY BOOKS FOR CHILDREN

DRAW THE IMAGE

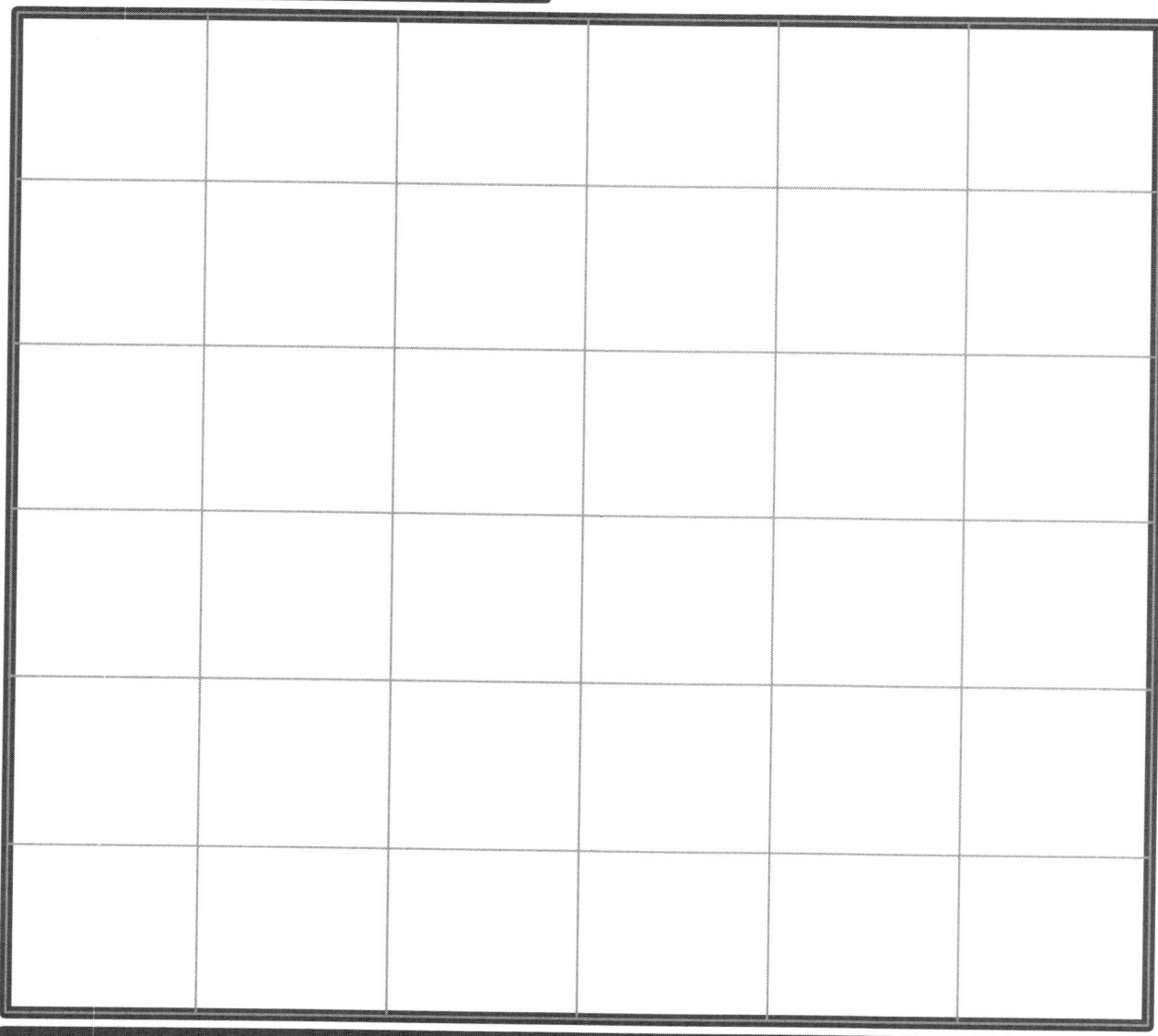

This is a Bleed Through Page If You Are Using a Coloring Marker or Pen!
Find Other Great Titles By searching for BoBo's Children Activity Books *on Your Favorite Book Retailer*
Amazon.Com | Barnes & Noble (BN.Com) | Books A Million (BAM.Com)

BOBO's
CHILDREN ACTIVITY BOOKS
COLORING, DRAWING & ACTIVITY BOOKS FOR CHILDREN

DRAW THE IMAGE

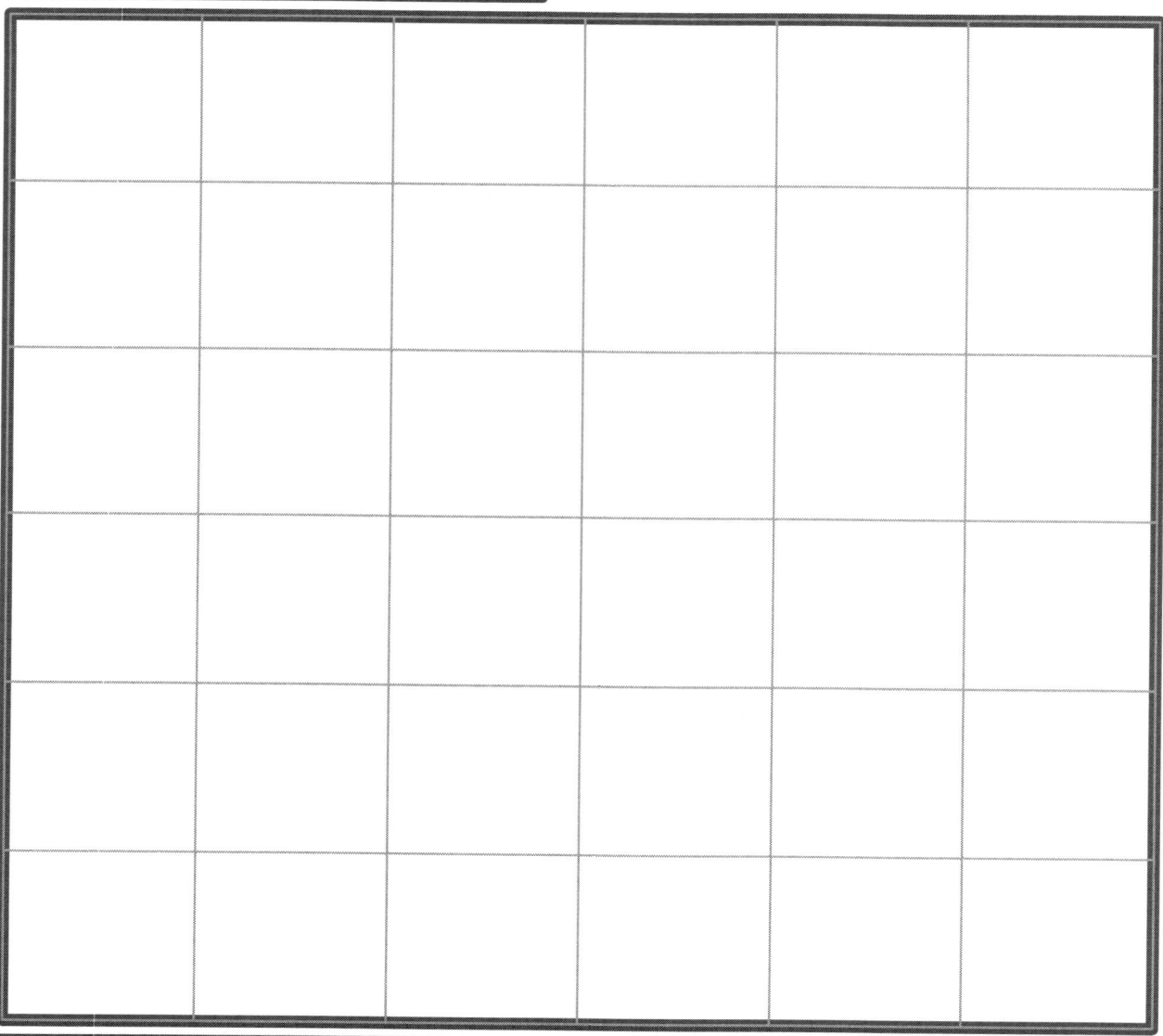

This is a Bleed Through Page If You Are Using a Coloring Marker or Pen!
Find Other Great Titles By searching for BoBo's Children Activity Books *on Your Favorite Book Retailer*
Amazon.Com | Barnes & Noble (BN.Com) | Books A Million (BAM.Com)

BOBO's
CHILDREN ACTIVITY BOOKS
COLORING, DRAWING & ACTIVITY BOOKS FOR CHILDREN

DRAW
THE IMAGE

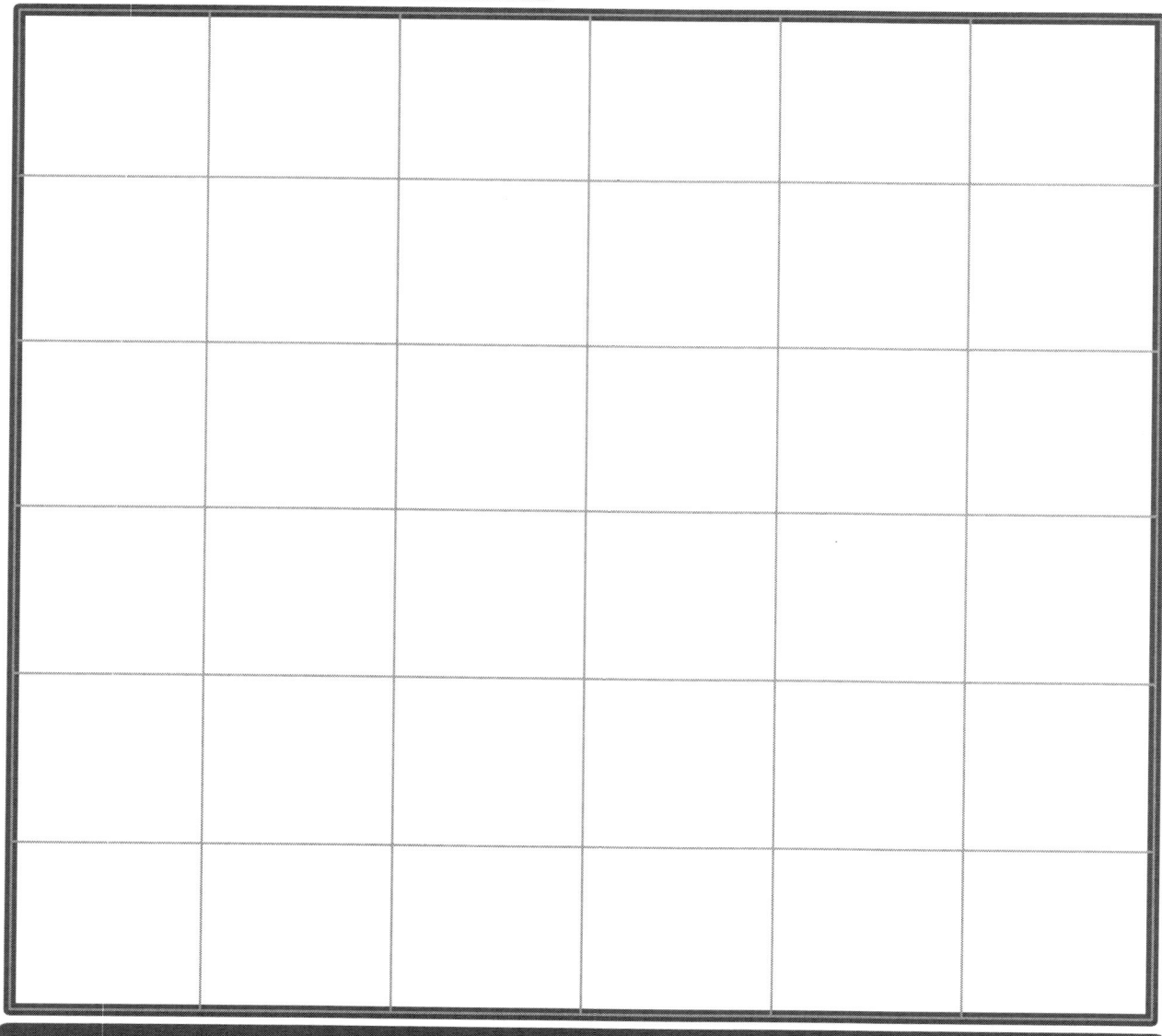

This is a Bleed Through Page If You Are Using a Coloring Marker or Pen!
Find Other Great Titles By searching for BoBo's Children Activity Books on Your Favorite Book Retailer
Amazon.Com | Barnes & Noble (BN.Com) | Books A Million (BAM.Com)

BOBO's
CHILDREN ACTIVITY BOOKS
COLORING, DRAWING & ACTIVITY BOOKS FOR CHILDREN

DRAW THE IMAGE

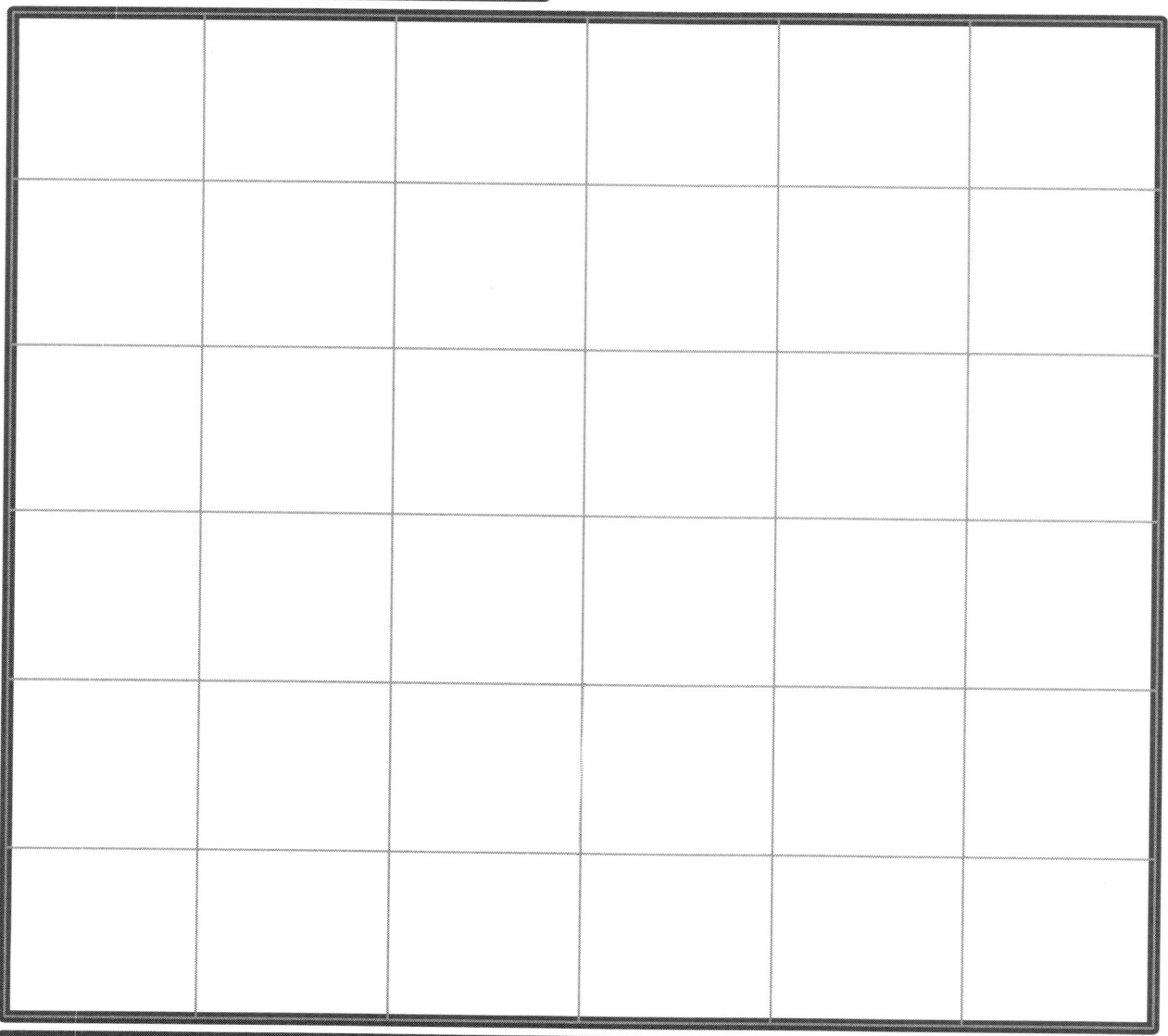

This is a Bleed Through Page If You Are Using a Coloring Marker or Pen!
Find Other Great Titles By searching for BoBo's Children Activity Books on Your Favorite Book Retailer
Amazon.Com | Barnes & Noble (BN.Com) | Books A Million (BAM.Com)

BOBO's CHILDREN ACTIVITY BOOKS

COLORING, DRAWING & ACTIVITY BOOKS FOR CHILDREN

DRAW THE IMAGE

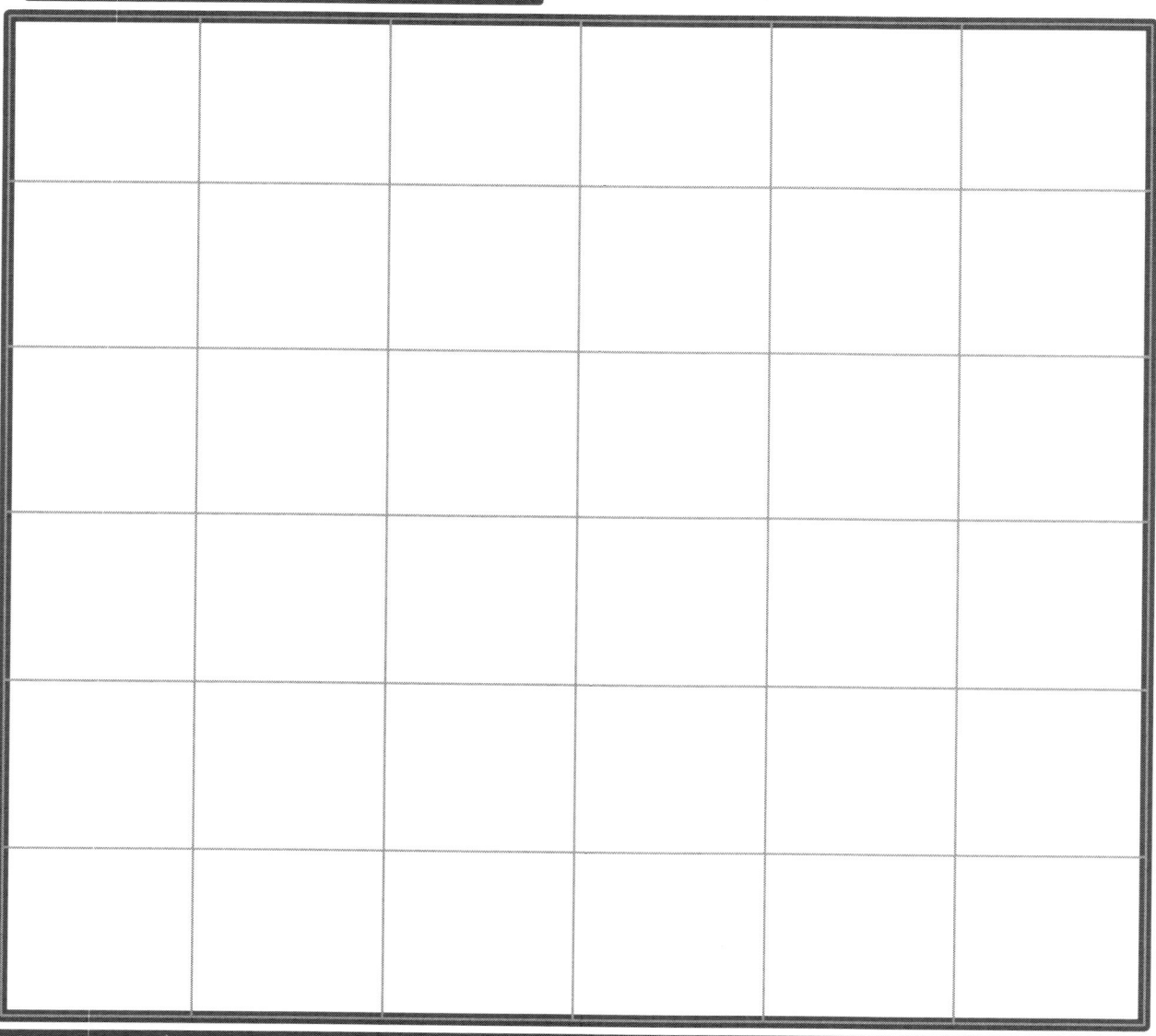

This is a Bleed Through Page If You Are Using a Coloring Marker or Pen!
Find Other Great Titles By searching for BoBo's Children Activity Books on Your Favorite Book Retailer
Amazon.Com | Barnes & Noble (BN.Com) | Books A Million (BAM.Com)

BOBO's
CHILDREN ACTIVITY BOOKS
COLORING, DRAWING & ACTIVITY BOOKS FOR CHILDREN

DRAW THE IMAGE

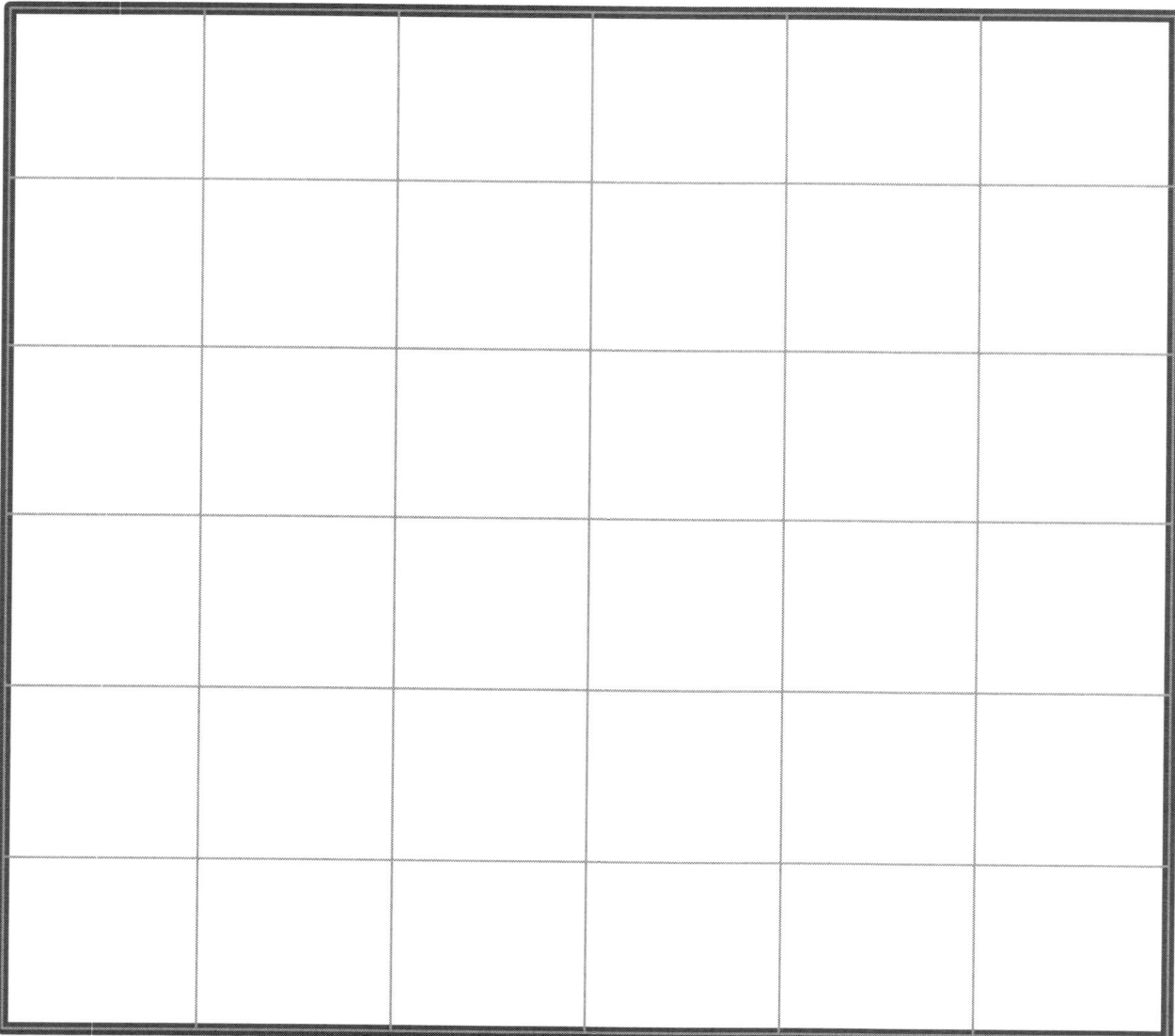

This is a Bleed Through Page If You Are Using a Coloring Marker or Pen!
Find Other Great Titles By searching for BoBo's Children Activity Books on Your Favorite Book Retailer
Amazon.Com | Barnes & Noble (BN.Com) | Books A Million (BAM.Com)

BOBO's
CHILDREN ACTIVITY BOOKS
COLORING, DRAWING & ACTIVITY BOOKS FOR CHILDREN

DRAW
THE IMAGE

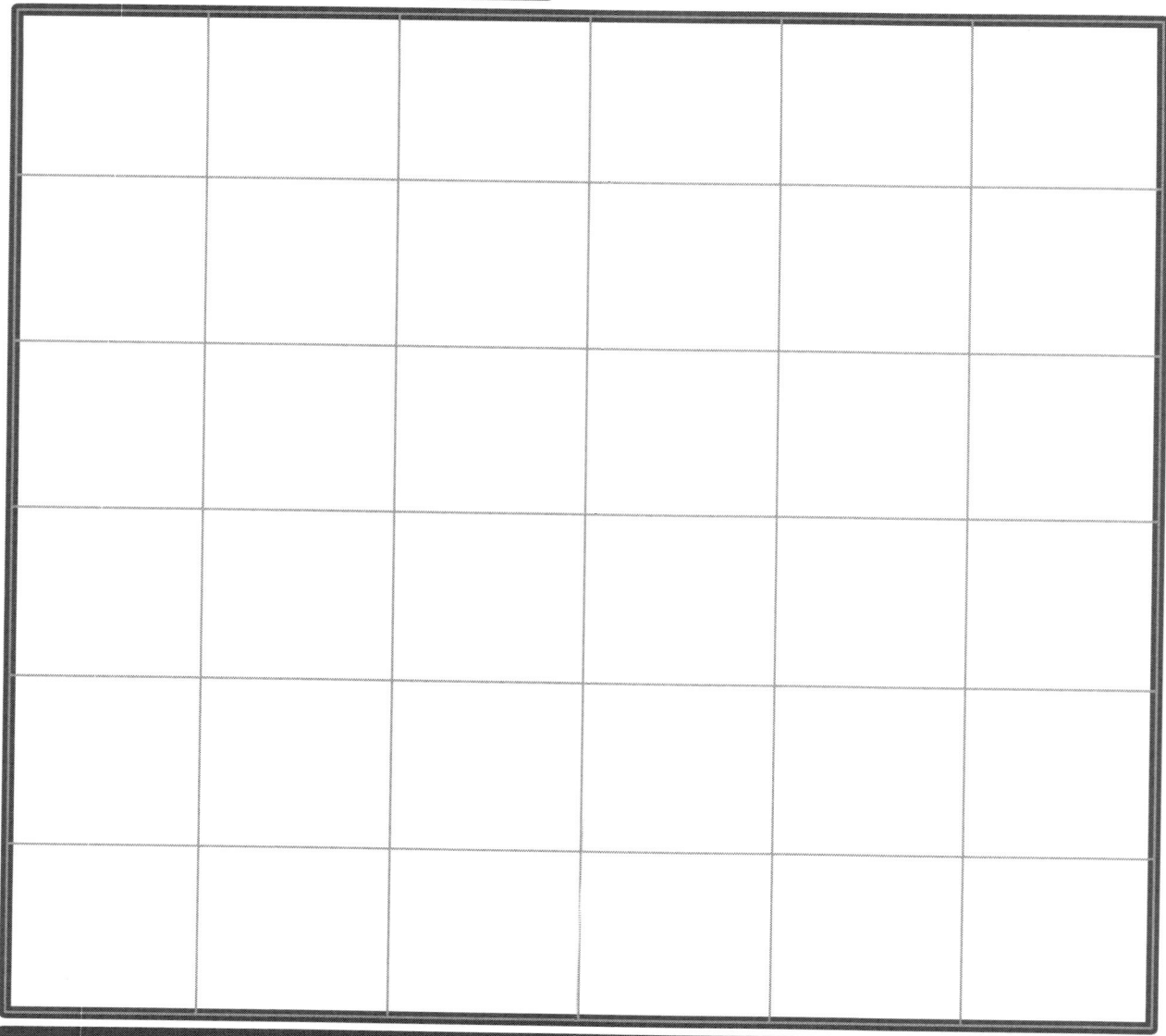

This is a Bleed Through Page If You Are Using a Coloring Marker or Pen!
Find Other Great Titles By searching for BoBo's Children Activity Books on Your Favorite Book Retailer
Amazon.Com | Barnes & Noble (BN.Com) | Books A Million (BAM.Com)

BOBO's
CHILDREN ACTIVITY BOOKS
COLORING, DRAWING & ACTIVITY BOOKS FOR CHILDREN

DRAW THE IMAGE

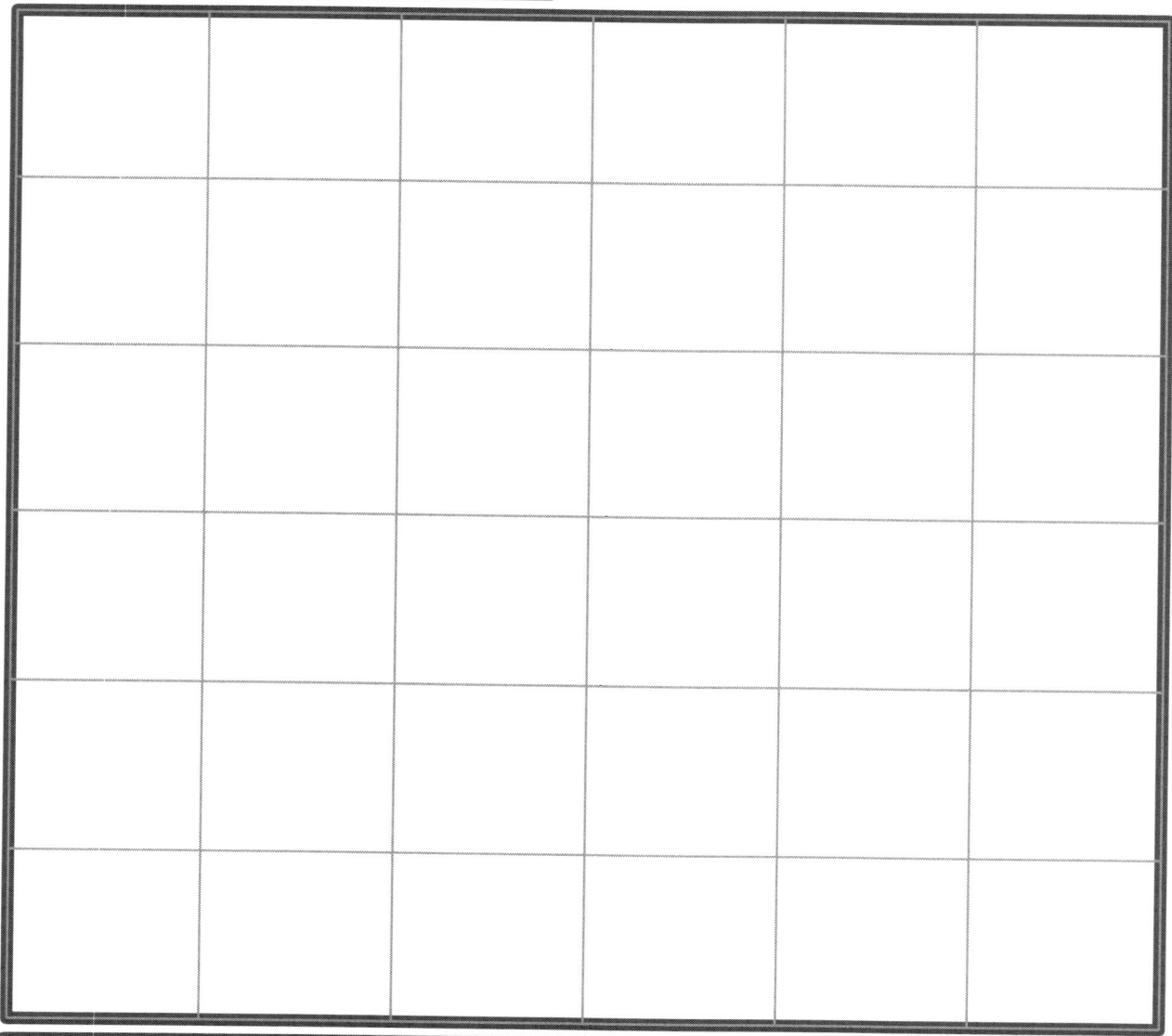

This is a Bleed Through Page If You Are Using a Coloring Marker or Pen!
Find Other Great Titles By searching for BoBo's Children Activity Books on Your Favorite Book Retailer
Amazon.Com | Barnes & Noble (BN.Com) | Books A Million (BAM.Com)

BoBo's
CHILDREN ACTIVITY BOOKS
COLORING, DRAWING & ACTIVITY BOOKS FOR CHILDREN

DRAW THE IMAGE

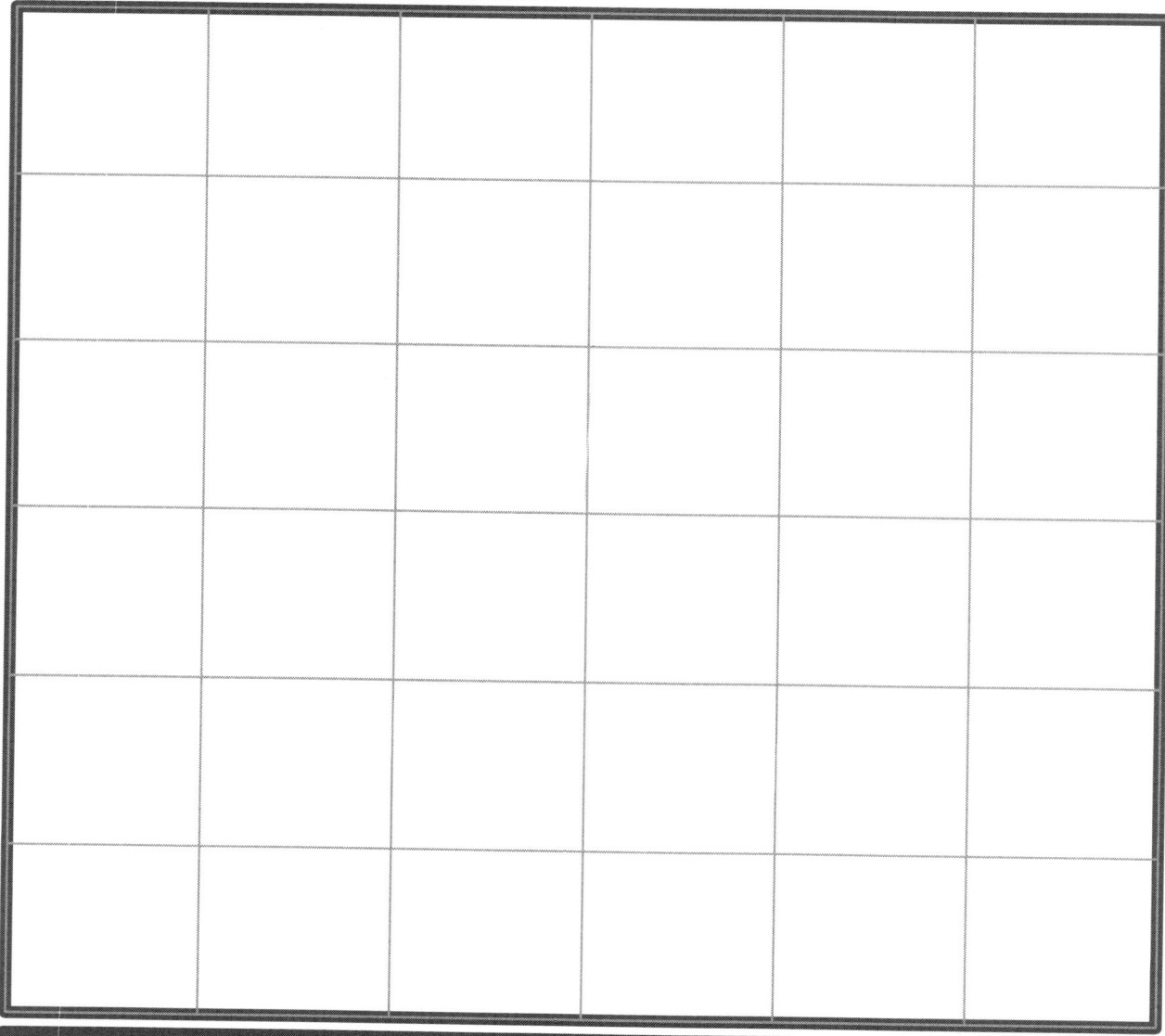

This is a Bleed Through Page If You Are Using a Coloring Marker or Pen!
Find Other Great Titles By searching for BoBo's Children Activity Books on Your Favorite Book Retailer
Amazon.Com | Barnes & Noble (BN.Com) | Books A Million (BAM.Com)

BOBO's
CHILDREN ACTIVITY BOOKS
COLORING, DRAWING & ACTIVITY BOOKS FOR CHILDREN

DRAW THE IMAGE

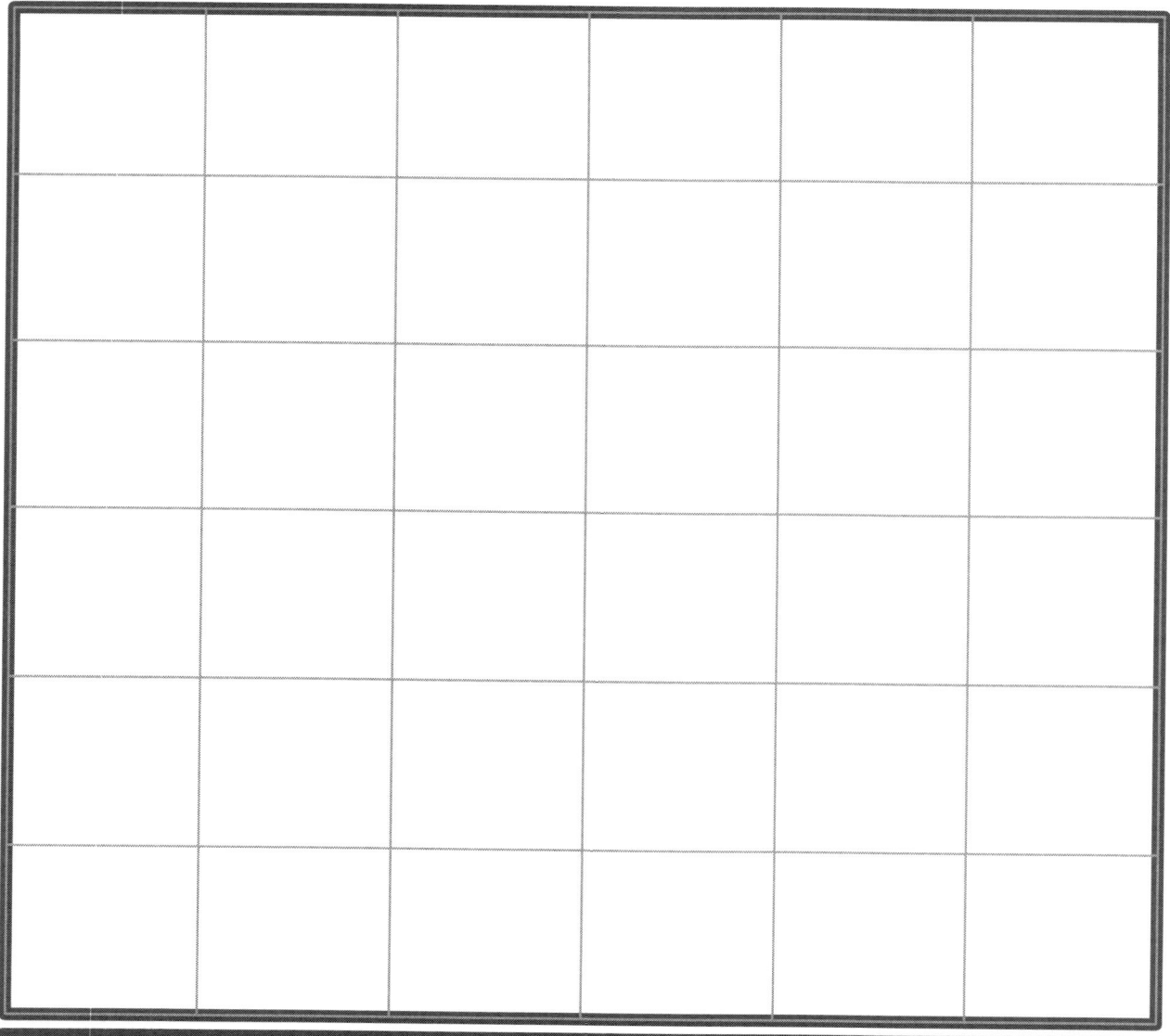

This is a Bleed Through Page If You Are Using a Coloring Marker or Pen!
Find Other Great Titles By searching for BoBo's Children Activity Books on Your Favorite Book Retailer
Amazon.Com | Barnes & Noble (BN.Com) | Books A Million (BAM.Com)

BOBO's
CHILDREN ACTIVITY BOOKS
COLORING, DRAWING & ACTIVITY BOOKS FOR CHILDREN

DRAW THE IMAGE

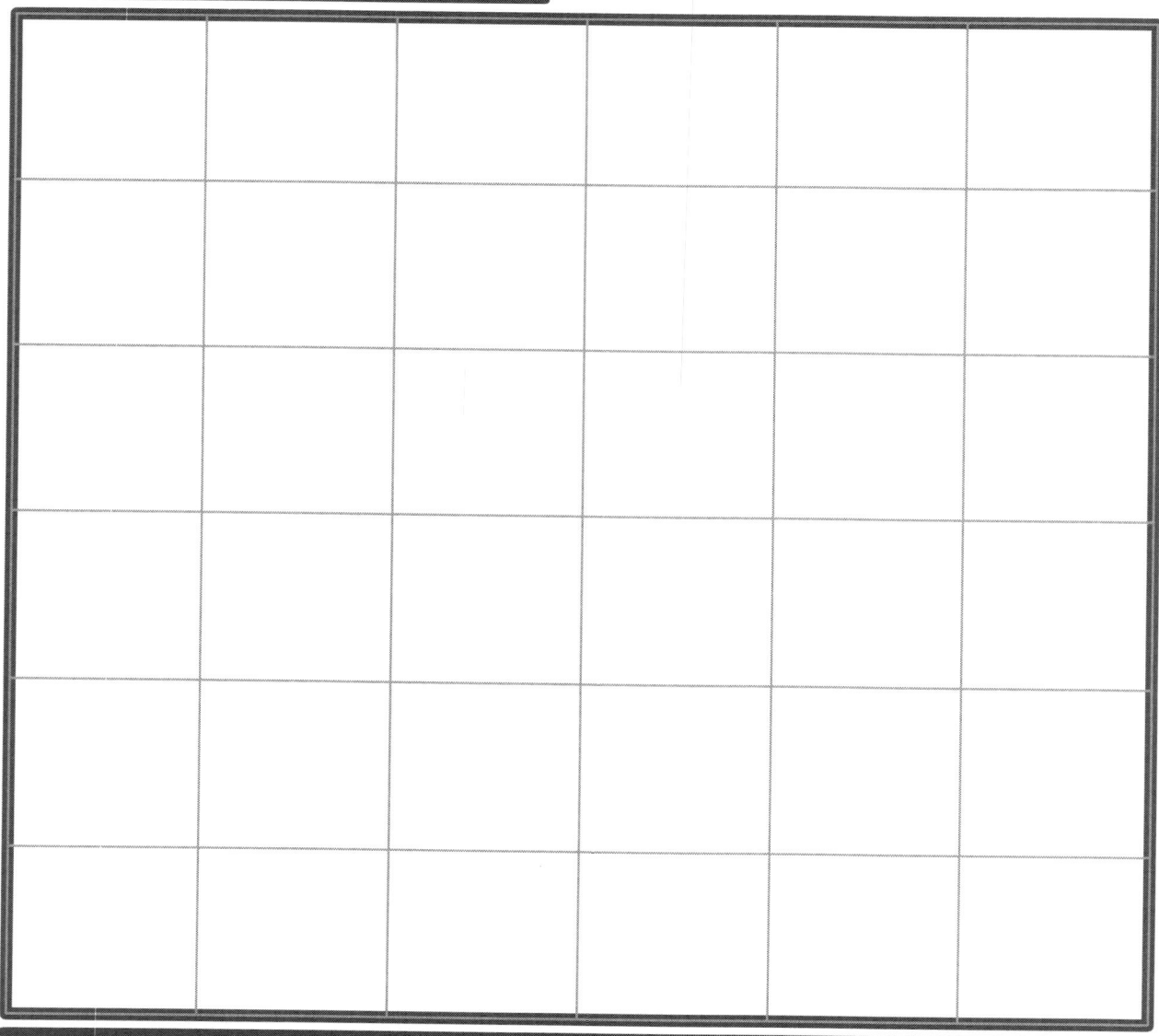

This is a Bleed Through Page If You Are Using a Coloring Marker or Pen!
Find Other Great Titles By searching for BoBo's Children Activity Books on Your Favorite Book Retailer
Amazon.Com | Barnes & Noble (BN.Com) | Books A Million (BAM.Com)

BOBO's
CHILDREN ACTIVITY BOOKS
COLORING, DRAWING & ACTIVITY BOOKS FOR CHILDREN

DRAW THE IMAGE

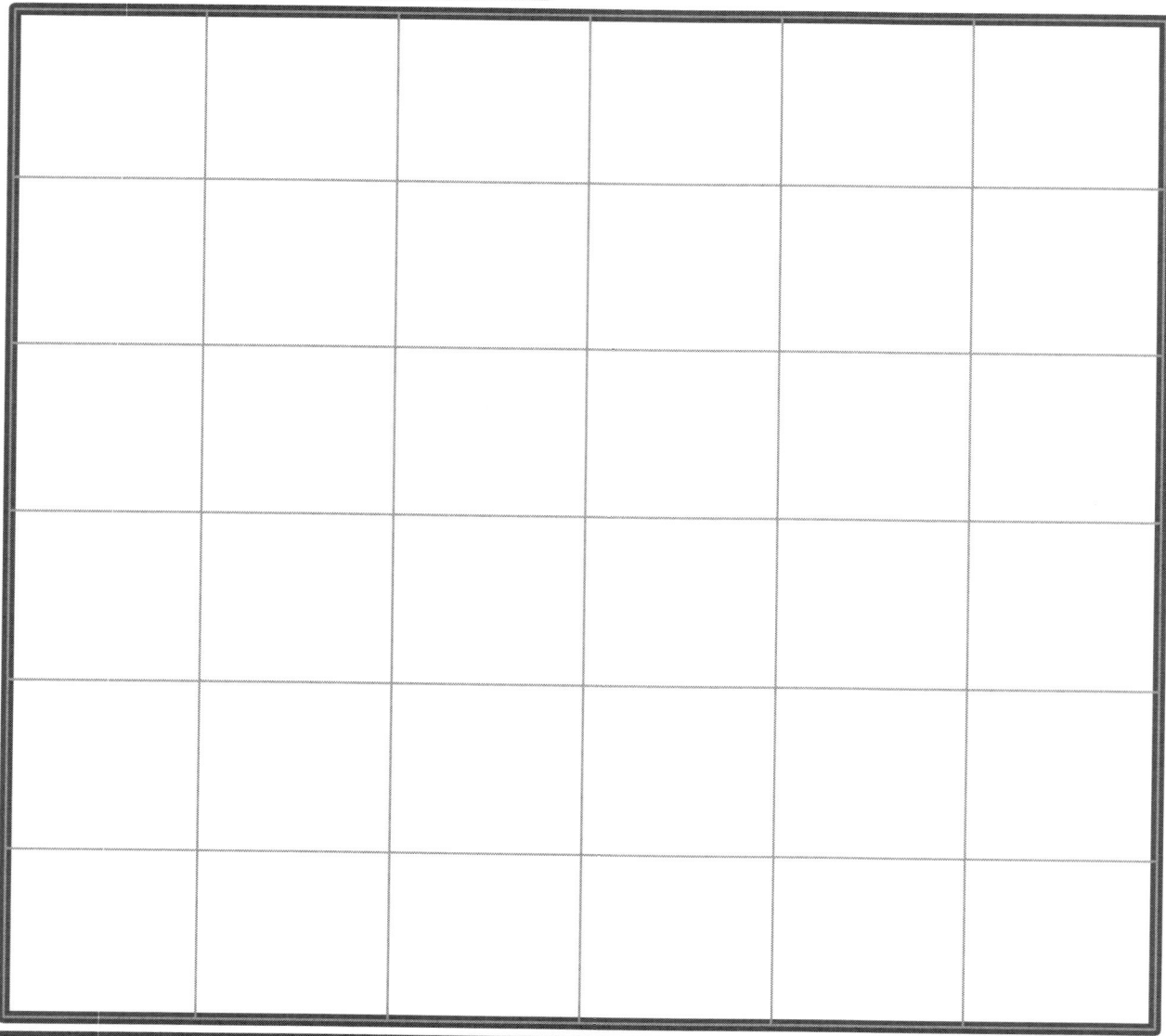

This is a Bleed Through Page If You Are Using a Coloring Marker or Pen!
Find Other Great Titles By searching for BoBo's Children Activity Books on Your Favorite Book Retailer
Amazon.Com | Barnes & Noble (BN.Com) | Books A Million (BAM.Com)

BOBO's
CHILDREN ACTIVITY BOOKS
COLORING, DRAWING & ACTIVITY BOOKS FOR CHILDREN

DRAW THE IMAGE

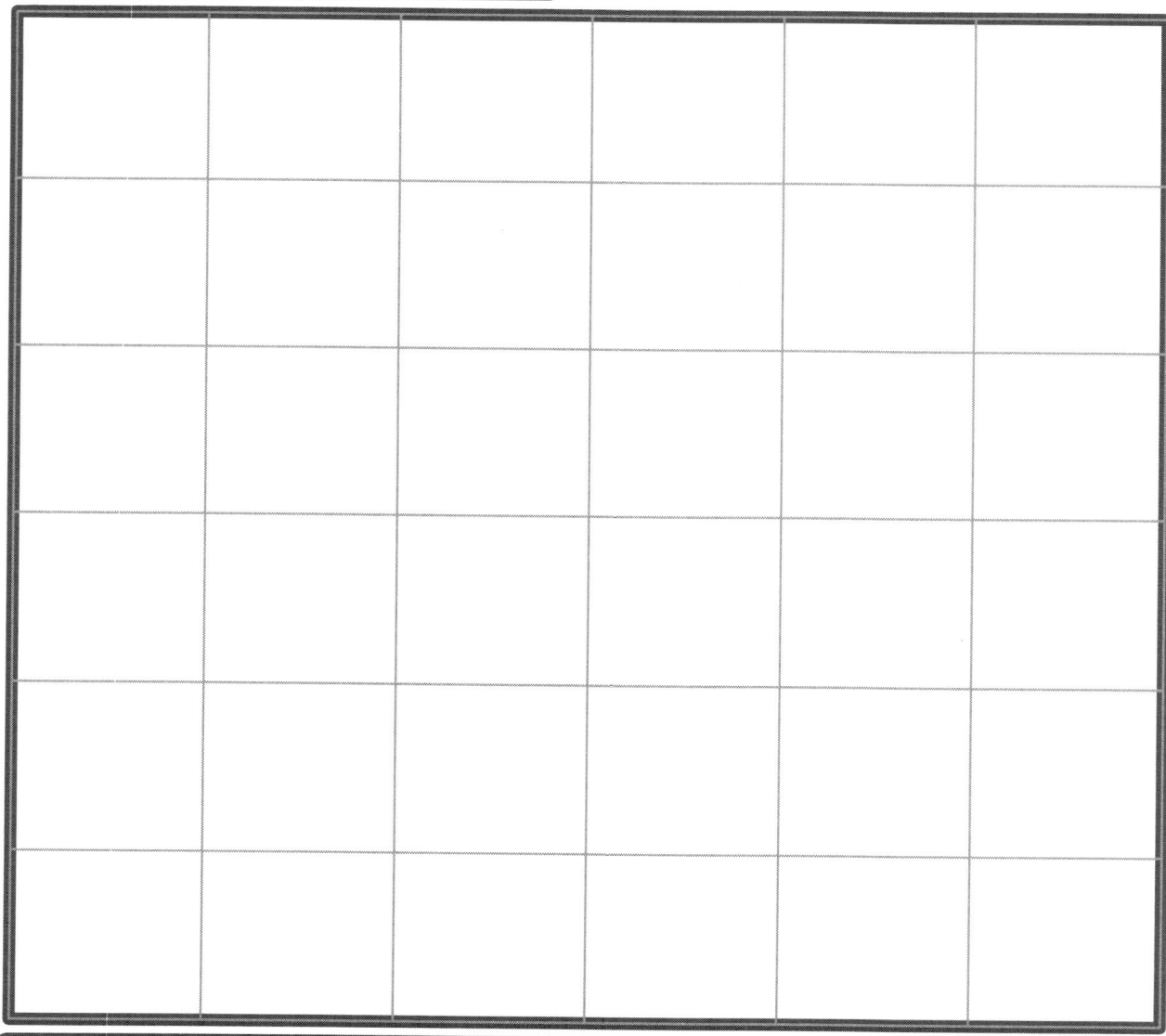

This is a Bleed Through Page If You Are Using a Coloring Marker or Pen!
Find Other Great Titles By searching for BoBo's Children Activity Books on Your Favorite Book Retailer
Amazon.Com | Barnes & Noble (BN.Com) | Books A Million (BAM.Com)

BOBO's
CHILDREN ACTIVITY BOOKS
COLORING, DRAWING & ACTIVITY BOOKS FOR CHILDREN

DRAW THE IMAGE

This is a Bleed Through Page If You Are Using a Coloring Marker or Pen!
Find Other Great Titles By searching for BoBo's Children Activity Books on Your Favorite Book Retailer
Amazon.Com | Barnes & Noble (BN.Com) | Books A Million (BAM.Com)

BOBO's
CHILDREN ACTIVITY BOOKS
COLORING, DRAWING & ACTIVITY BOOKS FOR CHILDREN

DRAW THE IMAGE

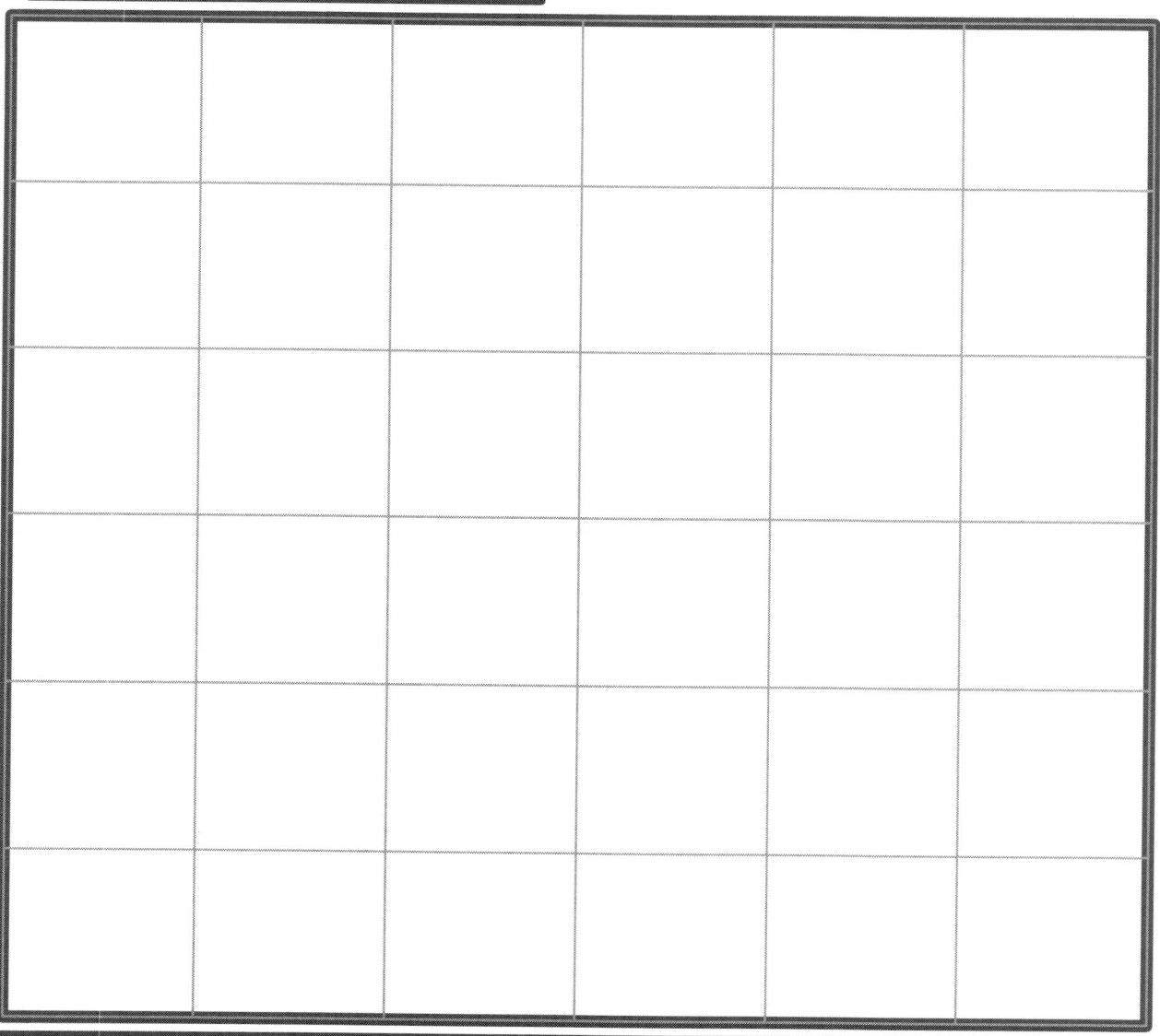

This is a Bleed Through Page If You Are Using a Coloring Marker or Pen!
Find Other Great Titles By searching for BoBo's Children Activity Books *on Your Favorite Book Retailer*
Amazon.Com | Barnes & Noble (BN.Com) | Books A Million (BAM.Com)

BOBO's
CHILDREN ACTIVITY BOOKS
COLORING, DRAWING & ACTIVITY BOOKS FOR CHILDREN

DRAW THE IMAGE

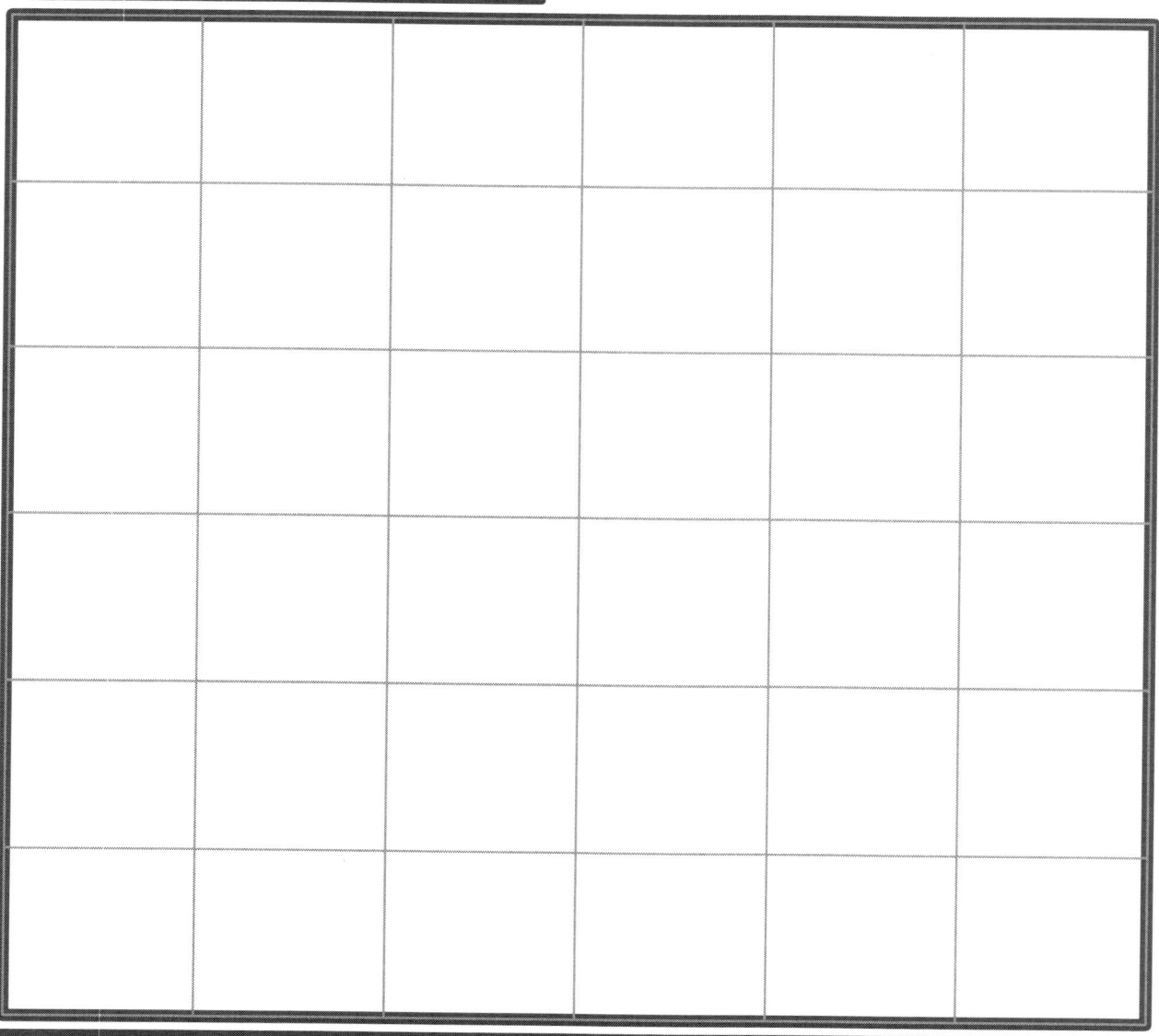

This is a Bleed Through Page If You Are Using a Coloring Marker or Pen!
Find Other Great Titles By searching for BoBo's Children Activity Books on Your Favorite Book Retailer
Amazon.Com | Barnes & Noble (BN.Com) | Books A Million (BAM.Com)

BOBO's
CHILDREN ACTIVITY BOOKS
COLORING, DRAWING & ACTIVITY BOOKS FOR CHILDREN

DRAW THE IMAGE

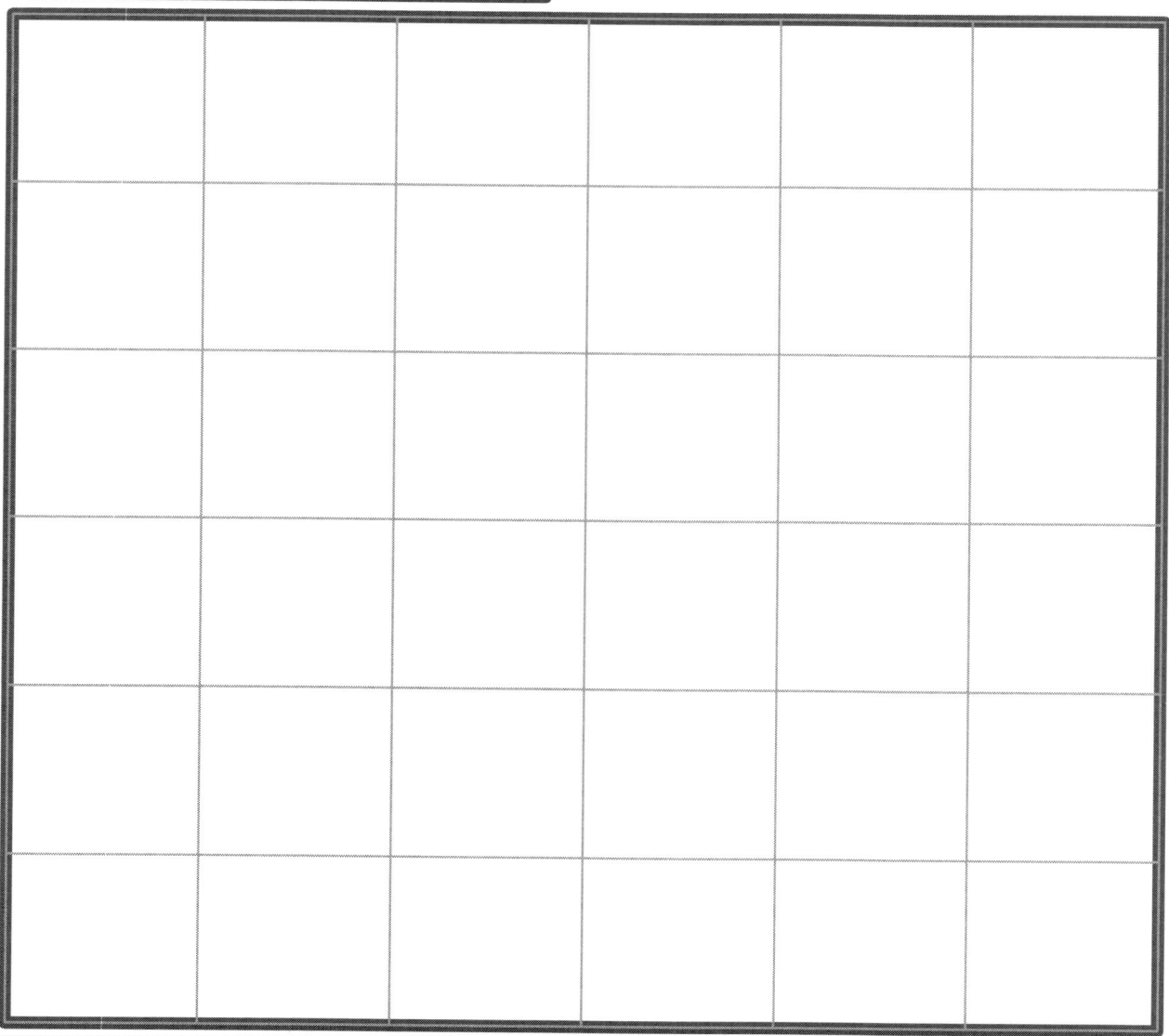

This is a Bleed Through Page If You Are Using a Coloring Marker or Pen!
Find Other Great Titles By searching for BoBo's Children Activity Books *on Your Favorite Book Retailer*
Amazon.Com | Barnes & Noble (BN.Com) | Books A Million (BAM.Com)

BOBO's
CHILDREN ACTIVITY BOOKS
COLORING, DRAWING & ACTIVITY BOOKS FOR CHILDREN

DRAW THE IMAGE

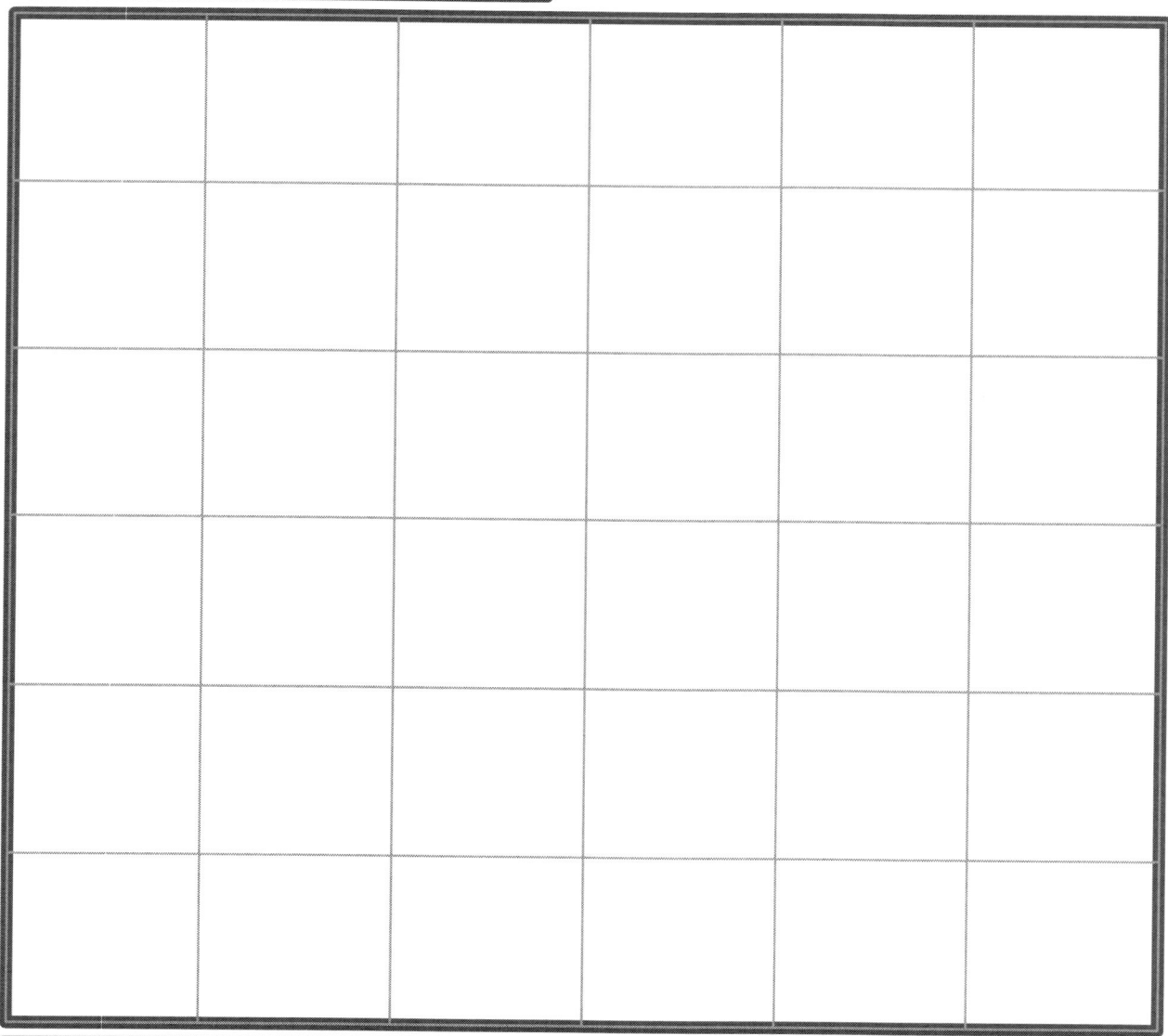

This is a Bleed Through Page If You Are Using a Coloring Marker or Pen!
Find Other Great Titles By searching for BoBo's Children Activity Books on Your Favorite Book Retailer
Amazon.Com | Barnes & Noble (BN.Com) | Books A Million (BAM.Com)

BOBO's
CHILDREN ACTIVITY BOOKS
COLORING, DRAWING & ACTIVITY BOOKS FOR CHILDREN

DRAW THE IMAGE

This is a Bleed Through Page If You Are Using a Coloring Marker or Pen!
Find Other Great Titles By searching for BoBo's Children Activity Books on Your Favorite Book Retailer
Amazon.Com | Barnes & Noble (BN.Com) | Books A Million (BAM.Com)

BOBO's CHILDREN ACTIVITY BOOKS

COLORING, DRAWING & ACTIVITY BOOKS FOR CHILDREN

DRAW
THE IMAGE

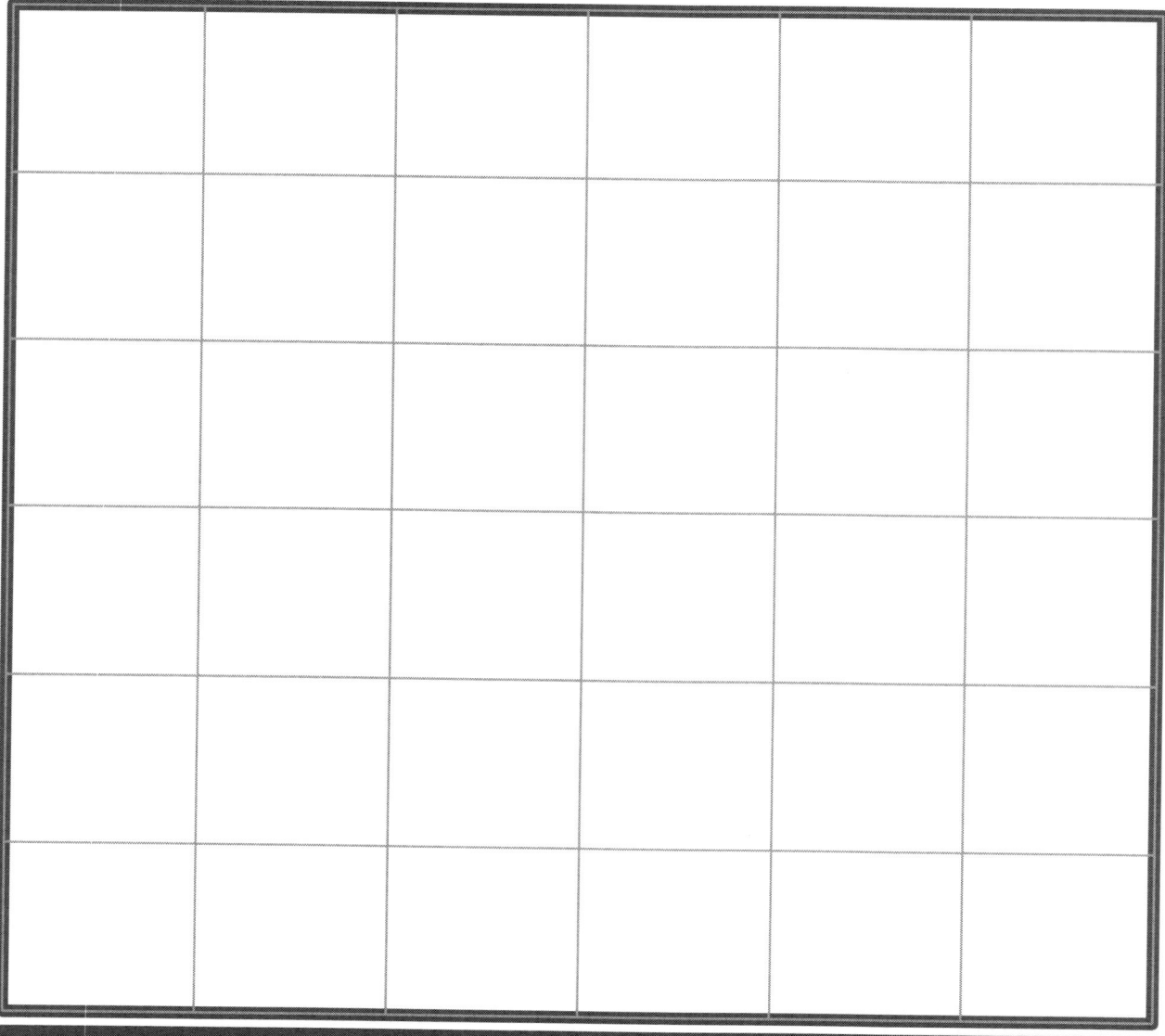

This is a Bleed Through Page If You Are Using a Coloring Marker or Pen!
Find Other Great Titles By searching for BoBo's Children Activity Books on Your Favorite Book Retailer
Amazon.Com | Barnes & Noble (BN.Com) | Books A Million (BAM.Com)

DRAW THE IMAGE

This is a Bleed Through Page If You Are Using a Coloring Marker or Pen!
Find Other Great Titles By searching for BoBo's Children Activity Books on Your Favorite Book Retailer
Amazon.Com | Barnes & Noble (BN.Com) | Books A Million (BAM.Com)

BOBO's
CHILDREN ACTIVITY BOOKS
COLORING, DRAWING & ACTIVITY BOOKS FOR CHILDREN

DRAW THE IMAGE

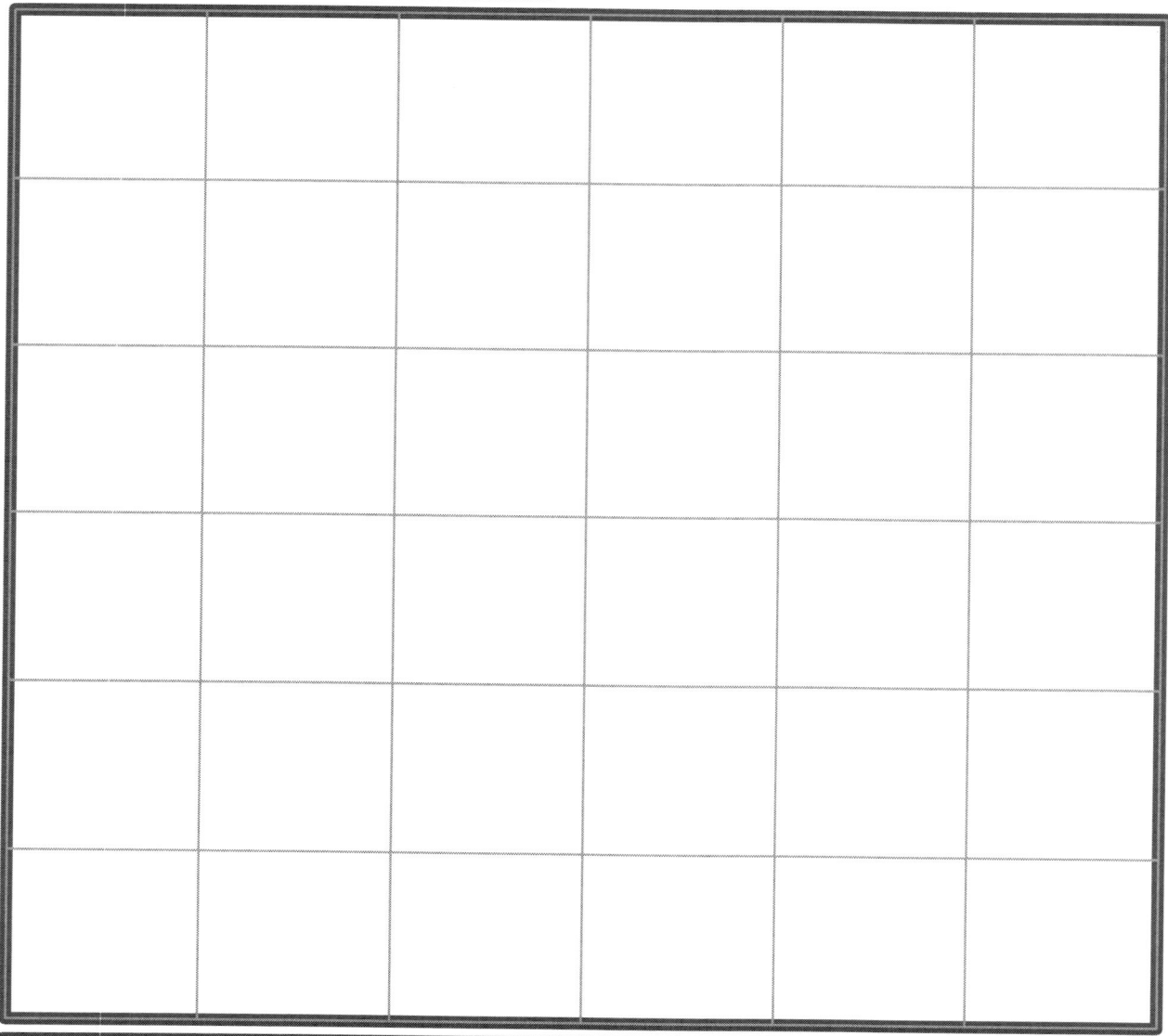

This is a Bleed Through Page If You Are Using a Coloring Marker or Pen!
Find Other Great Titles By searching for BoBo's Children Activity Books on Your Favorite Book Retailer
Amazon.Com | Barnes & Noble (BN.Com) | Books A Million (BAM.Com)

BOBO's
CHILDREN ACTIVITY BOOKS
COLORING, DRAWING & ACTIVITY BOOKS FOR CHILDREN

DRAW
THE
IMAGE

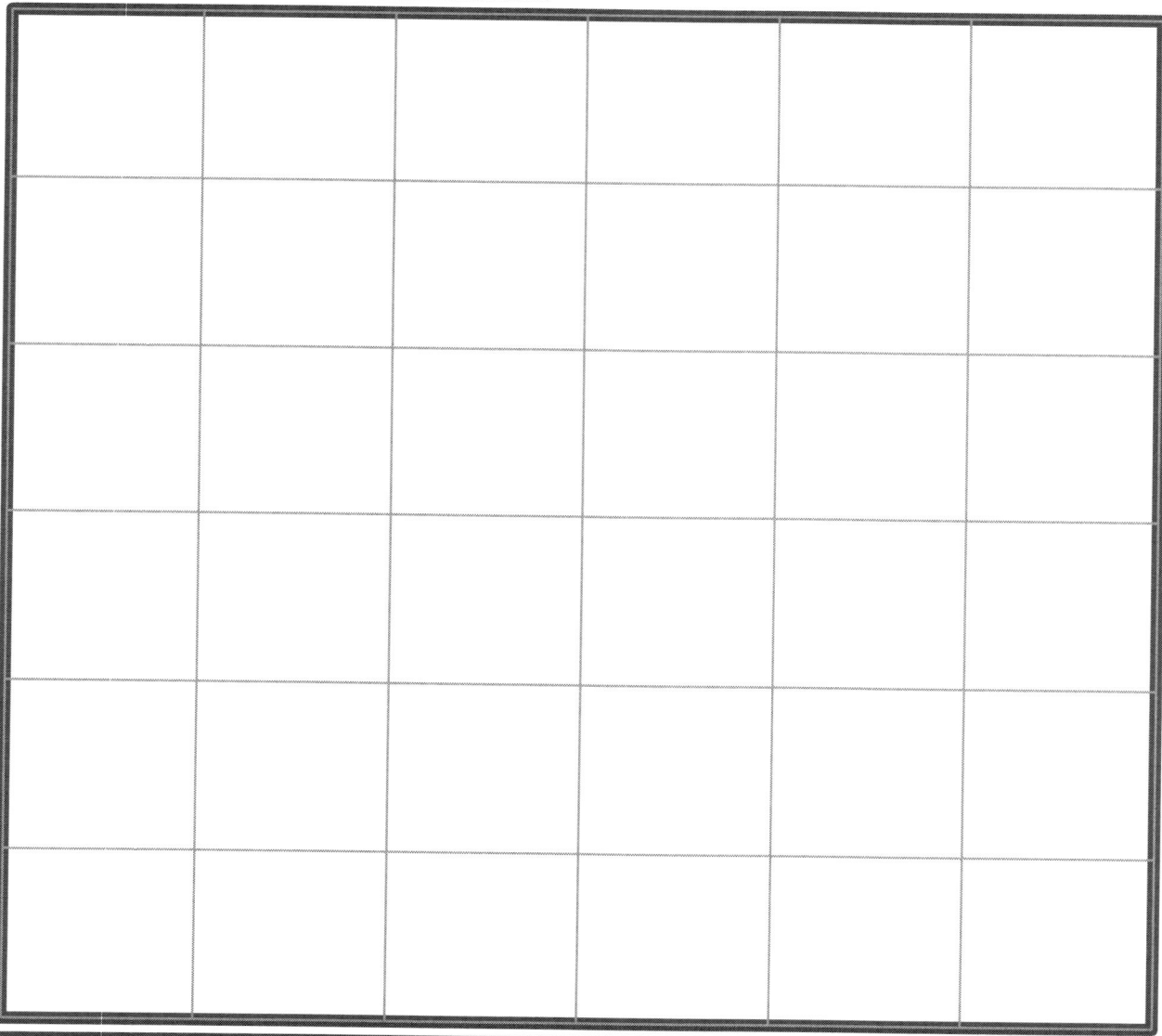

This is a Bleed Through Page If You Are Using a Coloring Marker or Pen!
Find Other Great Titles By searching for BoBo's Children Activity Books on Your Favorite Book Retailer
Amazon.Com | Barnes & Noble (BN.Com) | Books A Million (BAM.Com)

BOBO's
CHILDREN ACTIVITY BOOKS
COLORING, DRAWING & ACTIVITY BOOKS FOR CHILDREN

DRAW
THE
IMAGE

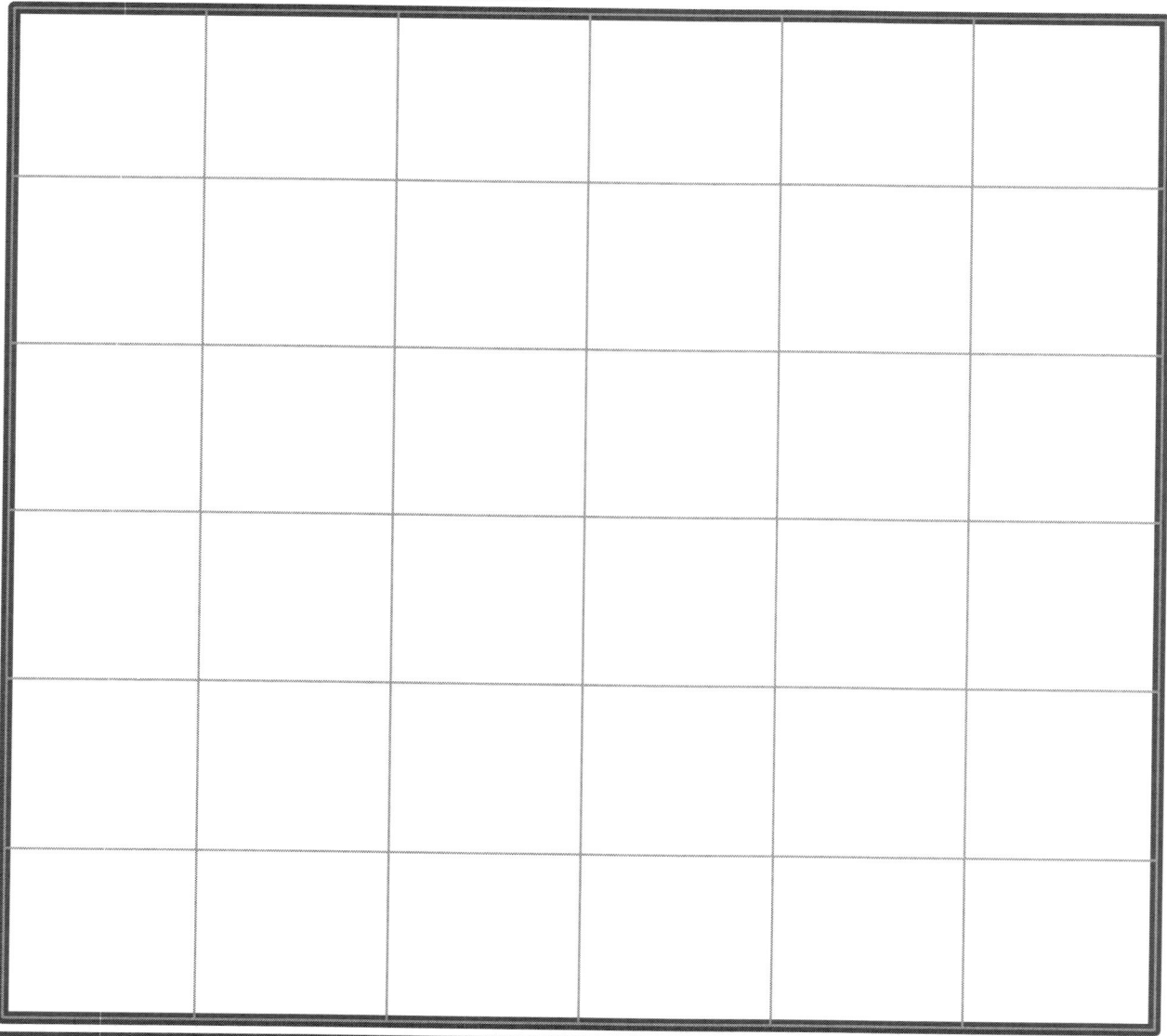

This is a Bleed Through Page If You Are Using a Coloring Marker or Pen!
Find Other Great Titles By searching for BoBo's Children Activity Books on Your Favorite Book Retailer
Amazon.Com | Barnes & Noble (BN.Com) | Books A Million (BAM.Com)

BOBO's CHILDREN ACTIVITY BOOKS
COLORING, DRAWING & ACTIVITY BOOKS FOR CHILDREN

DRAW THE IMAGE

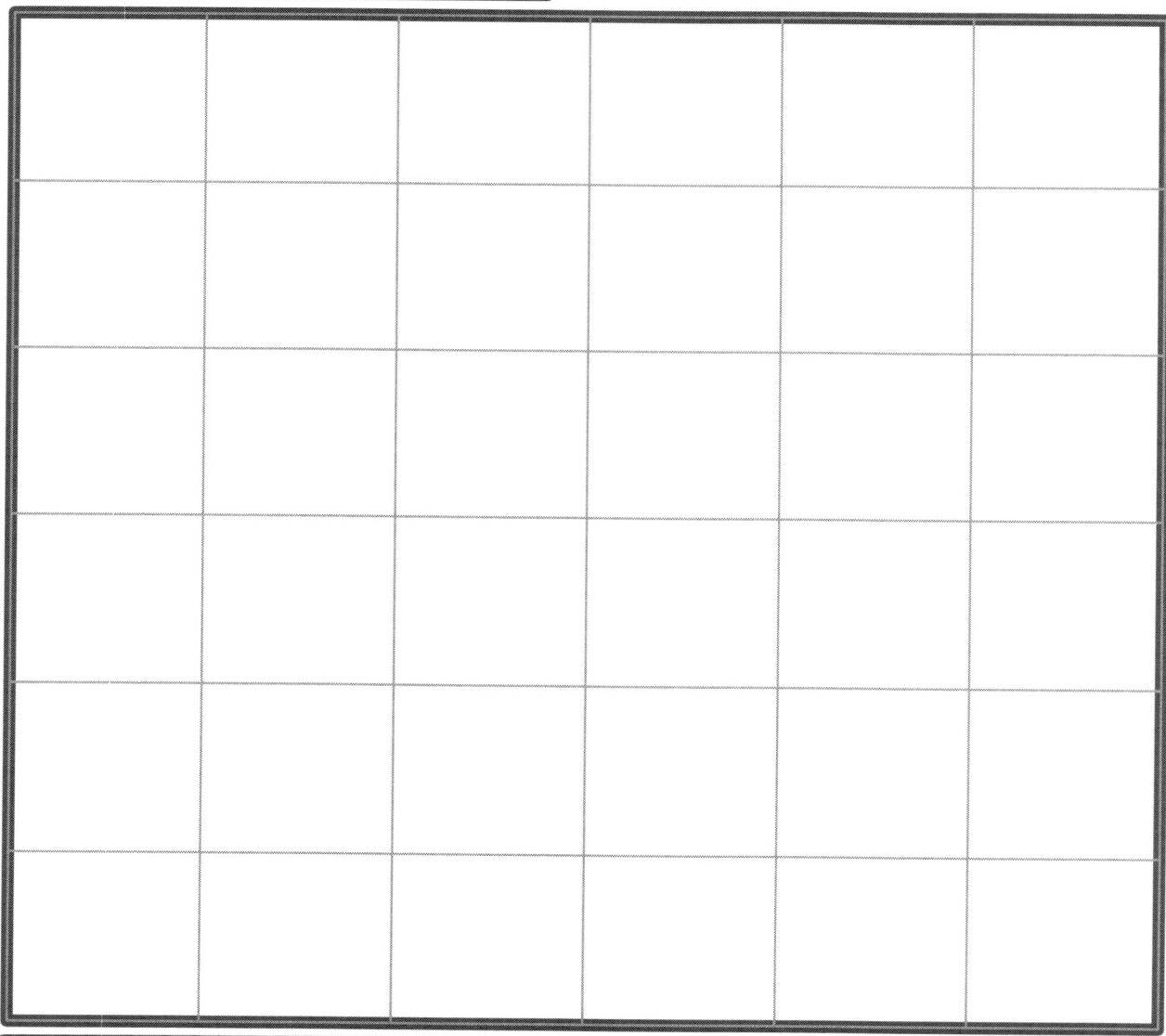

This is a Bleed Through Page If You Are Using a Coloring Marker or Pen!
Find Other Great Titles By searching for BoBo's Children Activity Books on Your Favorite Book Retailer
Amazon.Com | Barnes & Noble (BN.Com) | Books A Million (BAM.Com)

BOBO's
CHILDREN ACTIVITY BOOKS
COLORING, DRAWING & ACTIVITY BOOKS FOR CHILDREN

DRAW THE IMAGE

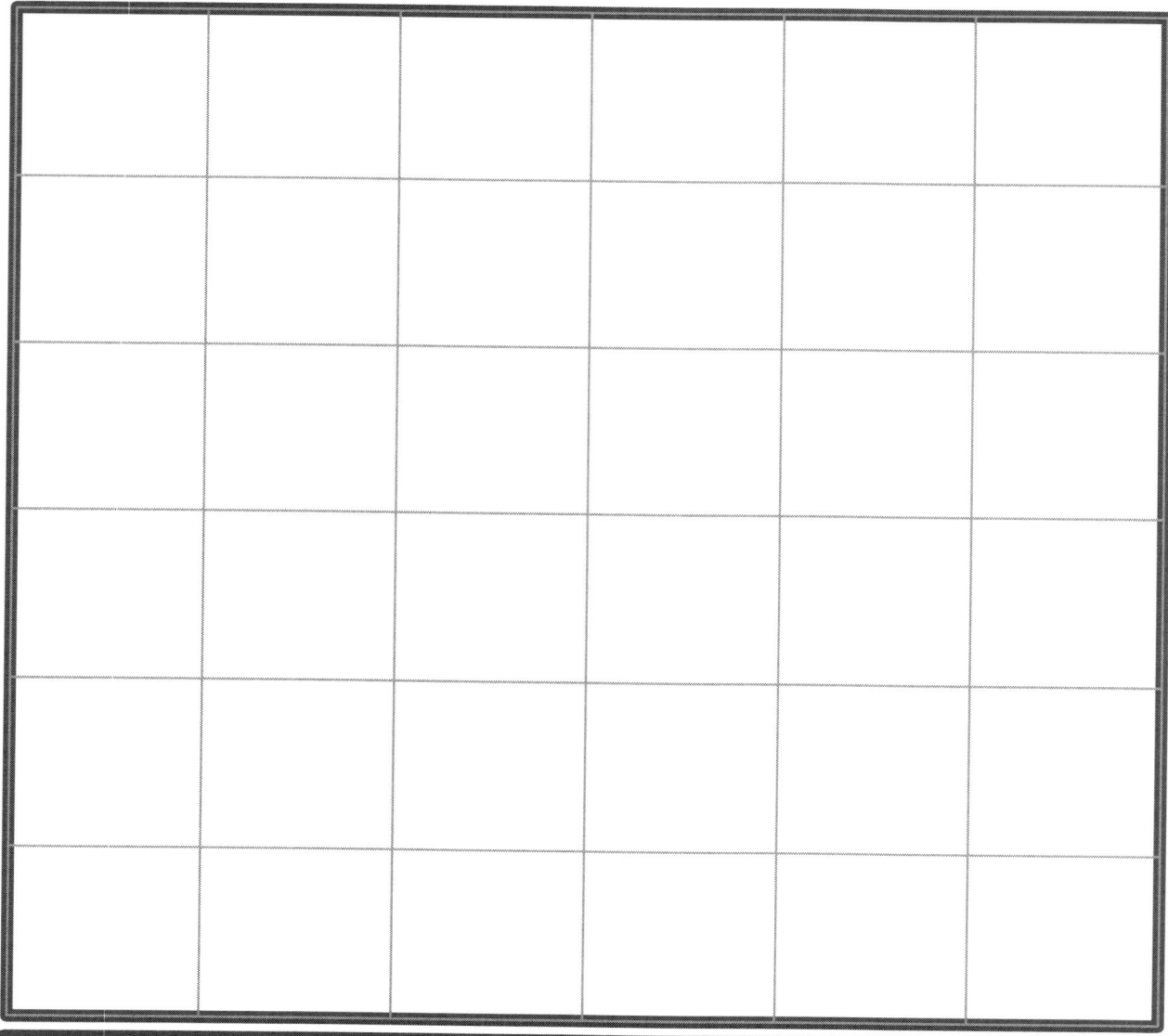

This is a Bleed Through Page If You Are Using a Coloring Marker or Pen!
Find Other Great Titles By searching for BoBo's Children Activity Books on Your Favorite Book Retailer
Amazon.Com | Barnes & Noble (BN.Com) | Books A Million (BAM.Com)

BOBO's
CHILDREN ACTIVITY BOOKS
COLORING, DRAWING & ACTIVITY BOOKS FOR CHILDREN

DRAW THE IMAGE

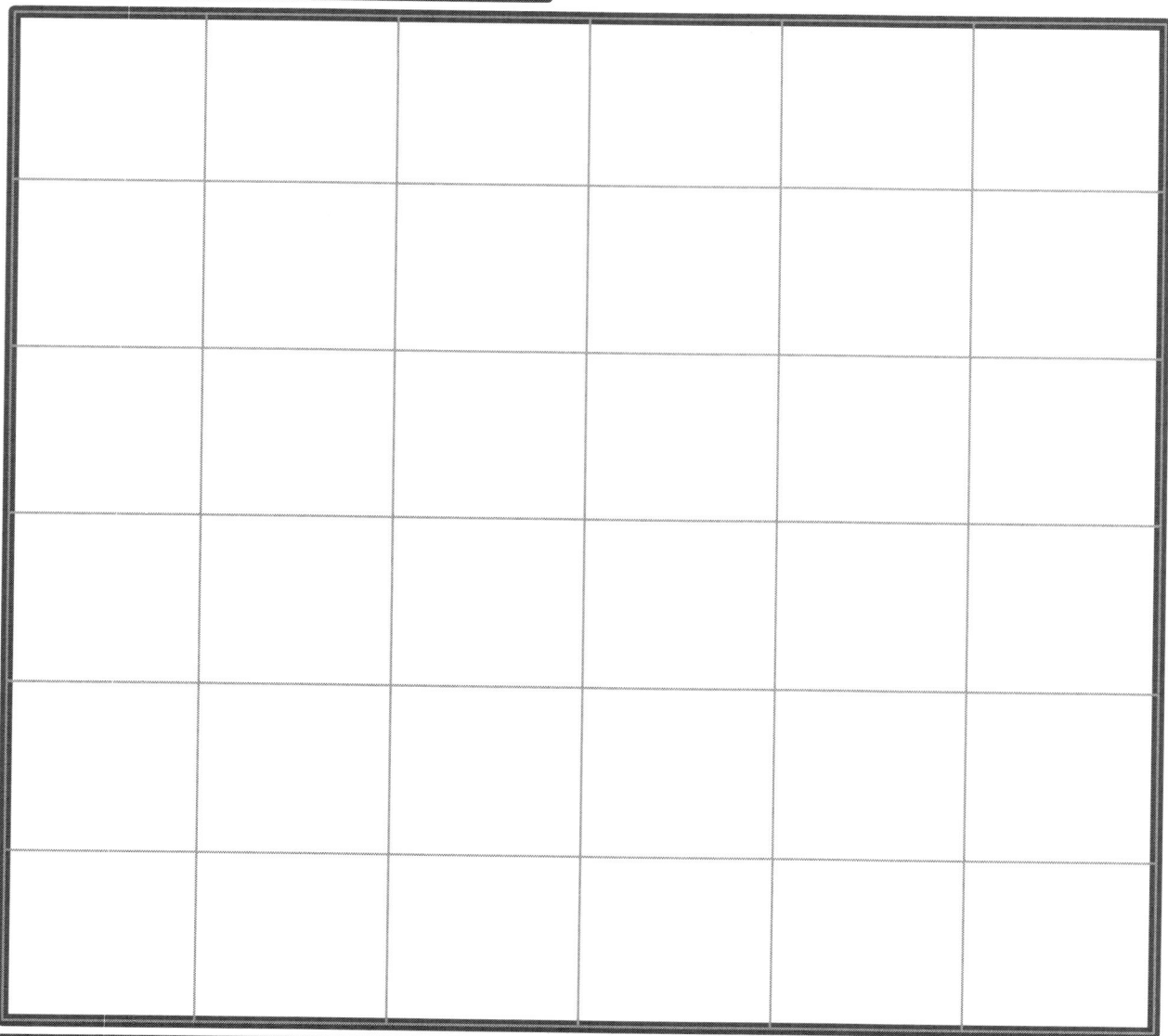

This is a Bleed Through Page If You Are Using a Coloring Marker or Pen!
Find Other Great Titles By searching for BoBo's Children Activity Books on Your Favorite Book Retailer
Amazon.Com | Barnes & Noble (BN.Com) | Books A Million (BAM.Com)

BoBo's
CHILDREN ACTIVITY BOOKS
COLORING, DRAWING & ACTIVITY BOOKS FOR CHILDREN

DRAW THE IMAGE

This is a Bleed Through Page If You Are Using a Coloring Marker or Pen!
Find Other Great Titles By searching for BoBo's Children Activity Books on Your Favorite Book Retailer
Amazon.Com | Barnes & Noble (BN.Com) | Books A Million (BAM.Com)

BOBO's
CHILDREN ACTIVITY BOOKS
COLORING, DRAWING & ACTIVITY BOOKS FOR CHILDREN

Printed in Great Britain
by Amazon